THE
WALKING DEAD
CHRONICLES
THE OFFICIAL COMPANION BOOK

THE WALKING DEAD

CHRONICLES

THE OFFICIAL COMPANION BOOK

PAUL RUDITIS

Foreword by Frank Darabont
Introduction by Robert Kirkman

ABRAMS, NEW YORK

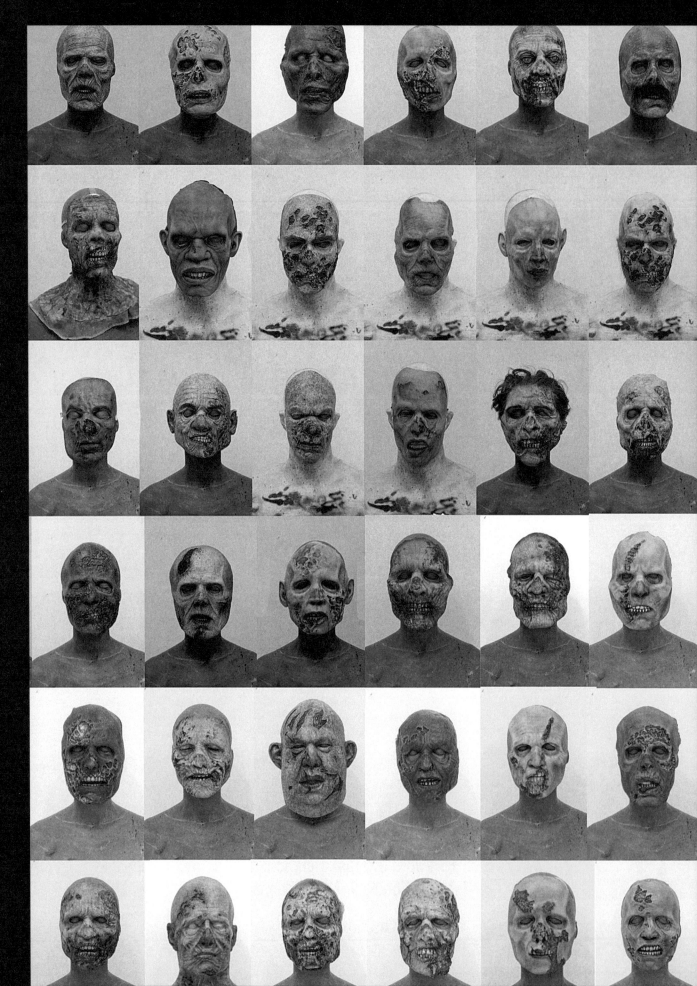

CONTENTS

FOREWORD

For me, it was instantaneous—it was very easy for me to want to do this show.

I'd been hankering to tell a zombie story for years. I love the zombie mythos, the whole George Romero world, and I'd been looking for an opportunity to play in that sandbox. And the timing seemed right—to this day, I'm quite surprised by the extent to which a previously little-known subgenre of horror, appealing only to geeks like myself, has blossomed into a concept with huge mainstream acceptance. Largely ignored by the broader public for decades, flesh-eating zombies were something we fans had all to ourselves, but over the last decade or so, zombies have lurched into the zeitgeist of popular culture in a way that I could never have anticipated. These days, I see grandmothers buying zombie books for their grandkids at big chain bookstores.

Finding the right zombie sandbox in which I could play remained elusive until the day I walked into a local comic book store and the first trade edition of *The Walking Dead* caught my eye. I saw it and thought, "Oh, cool. A zombie story. That's right up my alley." So of course I grabbed it and brought it home.

As I read the first issue that night, I was thinking, "This could make a really good TV show." By the second issue, I was thinking, "I'm going to call my agent tomorrow and see if the rights are available."

Robert's comic books had served up the very thing I'd been looking for. The next morning, I followed through, called my TV agent, and said, "What could be better for television than a really good, smart, character-driven ensemble show set in the zombie apocalypse?"

He thought it was a great idea. Then it took five years of rejections (plus joining forces with the estimable Gale Anne Hurd as my producing partner) before we could find any network to agree with us. Finally . . . thankfully . . . AMC saw the wisdom in the idea and said yes. My life has been nonstop zombies ever since.

A comic book is one thing, a TV series is another. Robert writes bleak, tough material. As a fan of the comic book myself, I want our show to visit the dark places Robert's already taken us, but there has to be a balance. It can't all be bleak, or the viewers will lose interest. Even Robert himself has expressed concerns about how certain twists and turns in his comic book would play out for a wider audience in a different medium over the course of, say, five years. Getting the tone right and maintaining it will be a very challenging and delicate balancing act. It'll definitely be a constant for us as long as the show runs—walking that tightrope of tone, having conversations with Robert every step of the way—because we don't want to veer too far in one direction at the expense of the other. This is a show that, fundamentally, wants to engage the audience and do what I feel the best television does: tell an extended story about the characters, people whose lives you want to follow for the long term. That's composed of countless smaller moments, too, not just the big "in-your-face" whammies.

For us to have turned out something that I'm proud of and tickled by and pleased with—something *I'd want to see*—is really a pleasure. If I heard somebody was doing a zombie show, *The Walking Dead* is exactly the show I'd hope for. So if I'm any barometer, if I'm any indication, I think we're off to a hell of a good start.

Best of all, the fans seem to agree, which makes me extremely happy and grateful.

—Frank Darabont

FRANK DARABONT *is the Academy Award– and Golden Globe–nominated writer, director, and producer of* The Shawshank Redemption *and* The Green Mile. *He developed* The Walking Dead *series for AMC and serves as executive producer, writer, director, and show-runner. He lives in Los Angeles, California.*

INTRODUCTION

As I type this, I'm sitting in a hotel in Atlanta, and shooting has just begun on the second season of *The Walking Dead* television show for the cable network AMC. I recently turned in the script for issue no. 88 of *The Walking Dead*, a comic book series for Image Comics/Skybound. McFarlane Toys recently released images of two new toy lines, one based on the show and another based on the comic book series. I just learned that the paperback collection of issues no. 79–84, titled *The Walking Dead Volume 14: No Way Out* will be featured on *Entertainment Weekly*'s Must List in next week's issue. I just looked over some art for *The Walking Dead* video game from Tell Tale Games. I just polished off the first *Walking Dead* novel, *Rise of the Governor*, with my cowriter, Jay Bonansinga. I saw a mock-up for a lunch box this morning. I approved a new T-shirt. There are coffee mugs in the works, a couple board games. And I recently turned down the opportunity to do *Walking Dead* cologne . . . It's all getting a little crazy.

Seriously. Cologne.

Thanks to the fine folks at AMC and Fox International, *The Walking Dead* is a worldwide phenomenon. The understatement of the decade, I think, is that *The Walking Dead* has outgrown me.

But isn't that what a creator wants, in the end? Creating something—a comic book, a novel, a TV show, a movie, whatever—is in many ways similar to having a child . . . and isn't the ultimate goal as a parent to give your child everything he or she needs to go out into the world on his or her own? The endgame of the whole process is watching them leave the nest, knowing they're prepared to deal with the outside world. In that respect, you don't create something only for yourself. You want as many people to enjoy it as possible.

So, if I look at it that way . . . it's kind of awesome that *The Walking Dead* has gone from being my thing, something I worked tirelessly on with my collaborators Charlie Adlard, Cliff Rathburn, and Rus Wooton to bring to the shelves of comic book stores and bookstores around the world, to this global sensation enjoyed by countless millions of people I will more than likely never meet.

The Walking Dead isn't just my baby anymore. There's an army of writers, artists, directors, musicians, sculptors, animators, set designers, costume designers, editors, producers, and actors involved in the various productions based on my original idea. It might seem like it would be kind of nerve-racking and overwhelming to have this many different people working on something you created in a room in your house when you were twenty-three, but it's kind of amazing to think about things growing into what they've grown into. I find comfort in knowing that in all cases, I've been able to hand-pick all the various people involved with *The Walking Dead*. My baby is in good hands.

All of which brings me to Frank Darabont. You may have heard of Frank. He's the writer and director of such classic movies as *The Green Mile* and *The Shawshank Redemption*. Frank is one of those filmmakers who will take their time between movies, picking the right projects to devote themselves to. He doesn't have a long body of work, but you can see that he pours his heart and soul into each project he undertakes. When Frank came along, it was like a breath of fresh air.

The truth of the matter is that Frank Darabont was not the first Hollywood muckety-muck to come after me for the rights to *The Walking Dead*. By the time he came along in 2005, I'd been fielding offers for about two years. Some came from names you'd recognize, but I'll refrain from mentioning them, as in most cases their ideas for what to do with *The Walking Dead* were just dreadful. Superzombies, zombie dog-beasts, heroic cannibals . . . in a lot of cases it actually seemed like people were trying to prove how they completely and utterly didn't "get" the source material.

And then Frank came along. It's funny—when I first got word from my manager that Frank wanted to talk to me, I thought, "That's weird, the *Shawshank* guy likes zombies?" This was because I didn't know Frank started out his career by writing movies like *The Blob*, *The Fly II*, and *Nightmare on Elm Street 3* (which actually work, in that order, as a kind of trilogy; you should try to watch them all in one sitting). And later, I would find out that Frank is probably the biggest Bernie Wrightson fan on the whole damn planet. Frank is entrenched in genre stuff. He loves horror and science fiction like nobody else.

But more important: Frank had read *The Walking Dead*.

And even more important than that: He got it.

My first phone conversation with Frank was pretty cool, I must say. As a comic book writer in Kentucky, I didn't talk to many big-time movie directors (some, but not many), and I remember being struck by how friendly and personable Frank was right

CONTINUED ▷

off the bat. It was like we were old friends talking about zombie movies. It wasn't a long conversation, but I got what I wanted out of it. Frank told me exactly what I wanted to hear:

"You're brilliant."

Only joking—what I really wanted to hear was:

"It's not about the zombies."

To me, that's the key to *The Walking Dead*, the simplest, most obvious thing about it, and yet Frank was really the first person to catch that right off the bat and, most important, embrace it. *The Walking Dead* is not an action zombie romp with intense gore and paper-thin characters meant only as cannon fodder—as much as I personally love that type of thing. *The Walking Dead* is a soap opera. It's a romance: a gripping tale of survival set against the most horrific worldwide tragedy one could think of, the dead walking and devouring the living.

The Walking Dead is something sad and tragic, a story that puts its characters through the wringer and sticks around to see what comes out the other end. And Frank, beat for beat, got all that. He saw *The Walking Dead* like I did. For the first time ever, I was face-to-face—or rather, voice-to-voice—with someone who seemed to care for *The Walking Dead* as much as I did. And for all the right reasons.

I knew we were a match right from the start, which was good, because we were in for quite the long haul when it came to making this TV show happen. In fact, I like to point out that Frank and I sort of languished with an unmade show until Gale Anne Hurd jumped on board, brought in AMC, and got this thing moving.

And the next thing you know, guys like Chic Eglee and Jack LoGiudice were brought in to write for the show. Greg Nicotero and KNB Effects Group were brought in to create the best zombies anyone had ever seen. Then Frank, Gale, and the folks at AMC assembled our legendary cast, and we were off to the races.

From there it was a *TV Guide* mention here, an international marketing stunt involving hundreds of zombies swarming cites all over the world there, and a few magazine covers and some amazing Internet coverage all leading up to a strong debut and, I'm told, an undisputed hit television show.

Now the books are flying off the shelves, I'm actually writing for the TV show while still working on comics, and my life has pretty much completely changed. Which is awesome . . . considering it was already pretty damn great to begin with.

So . . . I don't really know what I'm trying to say here other than THANKS. Thanks for buying this book and supporting the show, the comic, the whatever. Thanks for giving us a shot and making this crazy endeavor a success. Thanks for dressing up like a zombie sometimes or getting a crazy *Walking Dead* tattoo or naming your son Rick Grimes and all that other stuff. It's really awesome and flattering and it makes me want to try harder to continue making the comic and the show as good as they can be, because you deserve it.

The Walking Dead belongs to *you* now.*

(And if you were really looking forward to getting some *Walking Dead* cologne . . . sorry about that.)

−Robert Kirkman

* But I'm still going to keep my royalties, okay?

ROBERT KIRKMAN *is the* New York Times *bestselling author and creator of* The Walking Dead *and* Invincible. *Kirkman is a partner at Image Comics, where he founded the Skybound imprint, and is also a writer for and executive producer of AMC's* The Walking Dead. *He lives in Backwoods, California.*

ONE

WORLD-BUILDING IN COMICS:

THE CREATION OF *THE WALKING DEAD*

The Walking Dead has been unconventional since its inception, revealing a depth not always found in the pages of comic books. It has been called an exploration of the breakdown of society in a postapocalyptic world; a character study of a man pushed to the breaking point to protect his family; and even a commentary on a consumer culture forced to live a stripped-down existence without TV and iPads. Series creator Robert Kirkman centered *The Walking Dead* on a simpler core concept: It is the zombie story that never ends. "Every time you watch a zombie movie, the end of the movie is always the same," he laments. "It's either the last few people who survive ride off into the sunset in some way, or everyone dies."

He cites a certain abruptness usually associated with those stories in which a climactic final battle often springs out of nowhere, forcing the survivors to meet one of two preordained fates. And though he has been a fan of the genre most of his life, these pat outcomes left him wanting more. "There's never really been a story that continued with the characters who rode off into the sunset," he explains. "There's never been a continuing narrative that stayed in the world and followed the characters to their natural conclusion and saw them trying to survive for years and years in this [post]apocalyptic setting. It was definitely a book that I would have liked to have read, so I decided to make it because it didn't exist."

Kirkman's initial pitch for a long-form exploration of zombies was a science-fiction concept called *Dead Planet*. The story began in a mining colony on another world where an ore existed with properties that could reanimate human flesh. That ore eventually made its way back to Earth, and precipitated a futuristic zombie apocalypse. With that basic idea, Kirkman got to work realizing the vision. "It was going to be a fun book," he recalls. "Tony Moore, who drew the first six issues of *The Walking Dead,* was going to draw that book. . . . I got with him, and we worked together on designing the characters and everything."

Kirkman and Moore had been friends since childhood, when hanging out watching zombie movies together was one of their favorite pastimes. Later, when Moore was in art school,

Kirkman contacted his friend and suggested they team up on a comic book idea. This became their first official joint venture: *Battle Pope*, a satirical exploration of a hard-living pope called upon to save the world from demons, enlisting the help of Jesus Christ in the fight.

They released *Battle Pope* through Kirkman's newly created independent publishing company, Funk-O-Tron. The comic book ran for fourteen issues, and though it didn't set the comic industry aflame, it did help get Kirkman's foot in the door.

ABOVE: Cover art, by Tony Moore and Val Staples, for *Battle Pope* issue no. 1. *Battle Pope*, by Robert Kirkman and Tony Moore, launched in 2000 as the first title from Kirkman's fledgling Funk-O-Tron small press company.

PREVIOUS SPREAD: *The Walking Dead* issue no. 1 launched in October 2003 with cover art by Tony Moore.

Over the next three years, he wrote a handful of comics, including *Tech Jacket* with artist E. J. Su for Image Comics. The book ran for only six issues, but a character Kirkman introduced at the same time would become a mainstay in the Image Comics universe: Invincible, whose eponymous comic book launched with artist Cory Walker in early 2003.

At the same time Kirkman was developing *Invincible* for Image, he was also working with Moore on the five-page preview of *Dead Planet*. They pitched it to a few comic book publishers, including Image, but this was before the pop-culture boom in zombies, and the idea was not immediately embraced. Although Kirkman really liked the concept, he found there was nothing they could do with it.

"In hindsight, I'm really glad that it happened," Kirkman says. "I still wanted to do something with Tony Moore. I still wanted to do something that involved zombies. So I put my thinking cap on and tried to come up with a way that I could essentially do that book, but maybe try to make it appeal to publishers a little better." He killed the science-fiction aspect of the story and boiled it back down to the core concept: the zombie movie that never ends.

This edit was not the silver bullet to kill off the comic book industry's doubts regarding the series's marketability; zombies were still an unproven concept. But there was something in the revised pitch that brought a glimmer of interest from Image Comics, the publisher with which Kirkman worked most.

Image Comics had launched its line in the early nineties, created by a group of artists from Marvel Comics who had grown tired of turning over the rights to their own work to someone else. These writers and artists envisioned a new paradigm for the industry in which the comic book creators would maintain ownership and copyright on their work. Image grew into a company with several imprints, each putting out diverse subject matter befitting its various creators. This gave the company an opportunity to bring in new writers with unique ideas beyond the traditional super-hero comics. *The Walking Dead*, as it would come to be called, was one such idea.

The current publisher of Image Comics, Eric Stephenson, was the company's marketing director when Kirkman pitched his series. Stephenson recognized the creative spark within the concept, but it wasn't an easy sell for him. "There was no huge outpouring of support for zombie material at that point. We almost didn't pick the book up, because at that time, zombie comics didn't do particularly well. It was in no way a sure thing."

Danny Boyle's zombie film *28 Days Later* had only recently opened in the UK and was still months away from wide release in the United States. It was a year before Max Brooks's parody book, *The Zombie Survival Guide: Complete Protection from the Living Dead,* was to be published. Zombies were far from a sure thing for any publisher, yet there was definite interest in the series and in seeing what Kirkman could do with a never-ending zombie tale. But if Image was going to make a commitment to the project, some changes needed to be made. The revamped five-page preview Kirkman and Moore had created seemed a little too cliché to Stephenson. His comment led to the now familiar opening in which Sheriff's Deputy Rick Grimes wakes from a coma. But something was still missing.

"The initial reaction to *The Walking Dead* pitch was that it didn't have a hook," Kirkman explains. "That it was just a straight zombie story, and there was nothing really unique about it." At that point, he was fully invested

ABOVE: A revised page from the comic book pitch, with art by Moore, in which Rick has his first encounter with the titular walking dead.

OPPOSITE: Jumping right into the story, Rick wakes to a new world order on the second page of issue no. 1, alone in a hospital and as yet unaware of the dangers outside his room.

in telling a straightforward zombie saga without the additional bells and whistles. In fact, the idea was evolving into a completely stripped-down concept that explored a human drama more than zombies. But Kirkman knew that any hesitation could kill the idea, so he did what any writer would do when faced with waning interest from a publisher. He lied.

Kirkman looked back to his original pitch for *Dead Planet* and lifted enough of the idea to provide a hook for the new series without hanging it all on the science-fiction aspects. "I said the whole story was hinging upon a later reveal that it was aliens that caused the zombies and that this was part of a massive alien takeover. They're weakening the government's infrastructure by bringing the dead back to life, and then they're eventually going to swoop in and take over the planet."

Image bought into the plan, unaware that Kirkman never intended to follow through on it. His hope was that they would be so enamored with the initial offering that they wouldn't mind the deception. The dreaded call from Eric Stephenson came after the first issue arrived. Stephenson couldn't find any of the hints of alien involvement in the story line and asked if he was just missing the foreshadowing or if that was something that would be dropped in during future issues. It was time for Kirkman to come clean, admitting that he didn't think it was necessary to go down that path—luckily, Stephenson agreed.

The evolution of the comic was not entirely complete. The working title of the new pitch was not the one that would be launched. When

PITCHING THE COMIC BOOK

The Walking Dead Proposal

Story

Rick Grimes is a small town police officer in the state of Pennsylvania. He lives in a nice house out in the county with his wife, Carol and his son, Carl. Rick doesn't see much action, aside from target training he's never even fired his gun, he's by no means a hero. When the news hits that the undead are roaming the countryside committing acts of mass murder and eating their victims Rick must rise to the challenge to protect his family from the madness around him.

This book is about a man that will do anything to ensure that his family is safe. When private residences are deemed unsafe Rick takes his family on the road, in search of food, shelter, and something that at least resembles stability. We follow the Grimes family as they try to find a way to return to the normal life they once new. The first story arc will detail their trek across the state that results in their takeover of an abandoned high school. This high school quickly becomes a well-defended stronghold, as life in America turns into something not unlike medieval times. Once a safe base of operations is established Rick will lead an army on a quest to expand the safe zone, and eventually take back the planet… or at least try.

Format

The Walking Dead will be black and white, just like the best horror movies, in fact, even the covers could be black and white, further cutting down on the already minimal printing costs. The art will be completely gray-toned. Each issue will be a standard 22 pages. At the end of each year (sales allowing) a trade paperback collecting the 12 issues from the previous year will be released the same month as the first issue of the following year, providing a perfect jumping on point each year.(volume 1 shipping the same month as issue 13, etc.)

Contact
Robert Kirkman

ABOVE: Kirkman's pitch for *The Walking Dead* comic book series plotted a story line slightly different from the final comic—originally set in Pennsylvania and with Rick's wife named Carol—but one which still encapsulated the tone and core concept of the series.

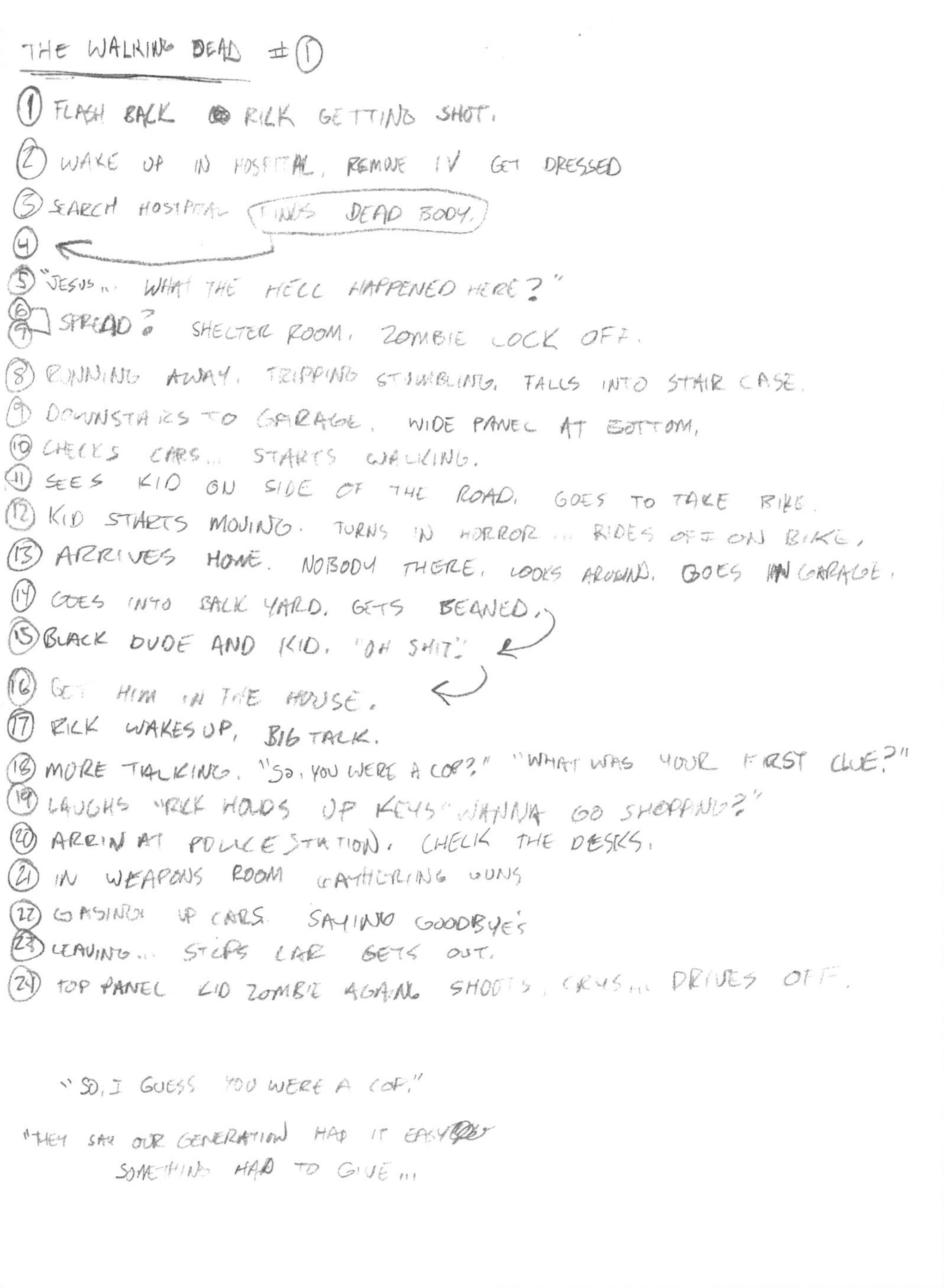

THE WALKING DEAD #1

1. FLASH BACK RICK GETTING SHOT.
2. WAKE UP IN HOSPITAL, REMOVE IV GET DRESSED
3. SEARCH HOSPITAL FINDS DEAD BODY.
4.
5. "JESUS... WHAT THE HELL HAPPENED HERE?"
6. / 7. SPREAD? SHELTER ROOM. ZOMBIE LOCK OFF.
8. RUNNING AWAY. TRIPPING STUMBLING. FALLS INTO STAIR CASE.
9. DOWNSTAIRS TO GARAGE. WIDE PANEL AT BOTTOM.
10. CHECKS CARS... STARTS WALKING.
11. SEES KID ON SIDE OF THE ROAD. GOES TO TAKE BIKE.
12. KID STARTS MOVING. TURNS IN HORROR... RIDES OFF ON BIKE.
13. ARRIVES HOME. NOBODY THERE. LOOKS AROUND. GOES IN GARAGE.
14. GOES INTO BACK YARD. GETS BEANED.
15. BLACK DUDE AND KID. "OH SHIT."
16. GET HIM IN THE HOUSE.
17. RICK WAKES UP, BIG TALK.
18. MORE TALKING. "SO, YOU WERE A COP?" "WHAT WAS YOUR FIRST CLUE?"
19. LAUGHS "RICK HOLDS UP KEYS" WANNA GO SHOPPING?"
20. ARRIVE AT POLICE STATION. CHECK THE DESKS.
21. IN WEAPONS ROOM GATHERING GUNS
22. GASSING UP CARS. SAYING GOODBYE'S
23. LEAVING... STOPS CAR GETS OUT.
24. TOP PANEL KID ZOMBIE AGAIN. SHOOTS, CRYS... DRIVES OFF.

"SO, I GUESS YOU WERE A COP."

"THEY SAY OUR GENERATION HAD IT EASY
SOMETHING HAD TO GIVE...

ABOVE: Robert Kirkman's handwritten plot outline for issue no. 1 of *The Walking Dead* provided a page-by-page breakdown of the comic.

Kirkman dropped the plan for *Dead Planet*, he needed to come up with a title that fit the new story. He wanted something that focused on his main influence: *Night of the Living Dead*, the 1968 George Romero film that reinvented the horror genre and introduced the modern idea of zombies. As luck would have it, the original theatrical distributor of that film had failed to include a copyright notice on the movie prints, which is required for a title to remain in copyright in the United States. As a result, *Night of the Living Dead* had entered the public domain. And that's what Kirkman wanted to call his new zombie epic.

Once again, executives at Image Comics stepped in with sage advice. Although the name recognition was certainly there, it limited what they could do with the series beyond comic books. Anyone interested in the rights to the story for film or television would have to change the title to avoid confusion with the original. Since the story was completely unconnected to the earlier film, it was better to choose a new title. Thus, *The Walking Dead* was born.

Although Kirkman's story was unique, there were some ties to the film he looked to for inspiration beyond just a bit of dialogue from the movie he had used in the revised pitch. The decision to have the interior art drawn in black and white for example was an artistic choice, as well as a financial one. "We thought it would be a way to pay homage to the work of George Romero on *Night of the Living Dead*," Kirkman explains, "and also to save a little money in the printing. I figured if sales did drop, I wanted to tell as much story as possible before they ended my

series, and we might be able to go a little bit longer if the printing was cheaper." Today, the cost of producing a full-color comic is not prohibitively more expensive than a black-and-white one, but Kirkman feels the art allows the comic to stand out on the shelves. It also has other benefits.

"*The Walking Dead* is very gory," Kirkman acknowledges. "There's a lot of horrendous stuff happening on the page. If you were seeing that in color, it would be that much more offensive. This really is a character study. It's not about the

ABOVE: As Moore's work on issue no. 2, page 13 reveals, the inherent gore of zombie battle is somewhat muted by the fact the comic is in black and white, but the violence still comes through.

OPPOSITE: *The Walking Dead* issue no. 2 was released in November 2003 with cover art by Moore.

ISSUE I

WIDE PANEL: Rick and Morgan are sitting in front of a fireplace in the living room. It's after dinner; they've got a fire going. They're just sitting in front of the fire chatting. Morgan's son is playing on the floor next to them...or drawing...or something.

SYNOPSIS: Sheriff's Deputy Rick Grimes is shot during a gun battle with an escaped prisoner and wakes from a coma some time later in a hospital that appears to be abandoned. But he is not alone. The barricaded cafeteria is filled with the living dead.

Rick escapes the hospital and returns home to find his family is gone. Missing photo albums suggest his wife, Lori, and son, Carl, fled with their most important memories. They may still be alive. As Rick steps outside, he takes a shovel to the head and loses consciousness. He later wakes to find Morgan Jones and his young son, Duane, are squatters in a neighbor's home, and they provide some answer about the new world order.

The trio makes a quick trip to the police station to load up on guns, supplies, and a police car to take Rick where he needs to go. He bids farewell to the Joneses and heads out to find his family in Atlanta, where he believes Lori would have gone to be with her parents. But first Rick makes a brief detour, returning to the half-missing torso of an undead woman he came across earlier to end her miserable existence.

shock value, and it's not about the gore. But you can't really do a story like this without the gore. By doing it in black and white, the gore recedes into the background so it isn't quite as jarring and doesn't really take center stage as much as it would if the book were in color."

The Walking Dead launched in October 2003 with an initial print run of roughly seven thousand copies. Image quickly discovered that its concerns about public interest in the series were unwarranted. "The first issue sold out immediately, and we went right back to press," Eric Stephenson recalls. "The second issue sold out right away, too, and then by the third issue, orders started going up. Orders have been on an upward arc ever since."

By that time, the film *28 Days Later* was a critical and commercial success. An impressive amount of buzz was also surrounding *The Zombie Survival Guide*, released only weeks before *The Walking Dead* launched. An unprecedented surge in popularity for the zombie genre was about to hit—and Kirkman and Moore's work would be leading the pack. But while *The Walking Dead* may have been one of the first major offerings in the zombie genre, many critics have noted that it isn't just the zombies that keep bringing readers back. "I'm really just doing a soap opera about survival," Kirkman admits. "Every now and then when there's a lull in the story, I'll just go 'Meh, I'll add a zombie attack.' I'm trying to pepper it in as little as possible, just because my main focus is always going to be on the characters." Those characters would be put through the wringer over the next several years.

The tale begins with a brief encounter on a country road in Kentucky. Sheriff's Deputy Rick Grimes is shot during an altercation with an

ABOVE: The opening panel of *The Walking Dead* issue no. 1 shows an atypical day in the pre-apocalyptic world in which Kirkman's characters lived.

escaped prisoner. It's the most action this small-town deputy has ever seen . . . until he wakes from a coma. He's in an abandoned hospital in a world that no longer resembles the one he knew before he lost consciousness. His family is gone. His hometown is largely deserted. And the dead walk the earth.

Over the course of the first six-issue arc, Rick discovers the terrifying reality of the world into which he has woken. He locates his family and his partner/best friend outside Atlanta, unaware of the relationship that has formed between his wife and his friend. He makes new acquaintances and watches some of them die, while they begin to look to him as their leader.

As winter sets in, the story moves beyond the outskirts of Atlanta to a gated community now overrun with zombies, a bucolic farm setting with a dark secret in its barn, and an unlikely prison sanctuary. Rick finds new friends, like the initially grounded Tyreese and the mysteriously lethal Michonne. He also makes a deadly enemy in a man known as The Governor. He experiences a loss at human hands that cuts deeper than any of the horrors the undead have visited on him.

The walking dead remain an ever-present threat in this new world order, but it is the human drama on which the narrative centers. As Rick will come to proclaim in issue no. 24, "*We are the walking dead!*" It is the humans, roaming through the broken world and struggling to survive, who serve as the backbone of the series. "It's really just a matter of making sure that people are invested in the characters, and that's really the story I want to tell," says Kirkman. "I want to know about how these people exist in this world and how they interact. How it's affecting them. How they treat each other and how they band together to survive. The zombies just kind of end up being a backdrop to make that story a little bit more interesting."

David Alpert of Circle of Confusion, a New York– and L.A.–based management and production company, honed in on the deceptively simple storytelling when he took Kirkman on as a client. "The thing about *The Walking Dead* is it's a zombie book without a gimmick," he says. "The thing that makes the story great is the characters and the[ir] relationships to each other. A lot of zombie things are 'Oh, we have fast zombies. Or we have talking zombies. Or we have zombies that can fly. Here's *our spin* on zombies.' The whole thing here is if there really was a zombie outbreak, it would play something like *this*. But, ultimately, it's really about how these characters react to this awful situation."

In Alpert's conversations with Kirkman, they discussed the zombies as an act of God or a natural disaster. "Sometimes it brings out the worst in people, like what happened with Katrina," Alpert says. "Or sometimes it brings out the best in people. When people sort of rally together and support each other and come to each other's aid. So, you're looking at how people react to peril and life-threatening situations, as opposed to just dealing with zombies."

The subject matter of *The Walking Dead* gets as dark as any other exploration of a post-apocalyptic world. Kirkman holds nothing back in his approach to his characters and their world. It is something that the audience has come to expect, even when it takes its darkest turns, like unexpected deaths and the now-infamous torture scenes involving Michonne and The Governor.

Admittedly, this darkness isn't for everyone. Publisher Eric Stephenson recalls a particularly affecting encounter he once had with a fan: "Years back, a guy pulled me aside at a comic book convention and said that he really loved the book initially, but that the more he read, the more it struck him as a story completely devoid of any kind of hope. He said he had to give it up, because it kept him awake at night, mulling over the utter hopelessness of it all."

Devoted readers might disagree with that interpretation. For some, the thing that keeps bringing them back is the hope they have for Rick to survive and find a safe haven. After dozens of issues and countless horrors, Rick Grimes has likely passed the point of ever achieving a "happily ever after," but the audience is deeply invested in seeing how events play out as the series approaches one hundred issues and beyond.

ISSUE 2

WIDE PANEL: Close on Rick, wiping his face and looking up at Glenn.

SYNOPSIS: Rick's police cruiser runs out of gas after he finds nothing but empty filling stations on the road to Atlanta. He goes to a local farmhouse for help, but comes across a family that has taken their own lives inside. Rick confiscates their horse to take him the rest of the way on his lonely journey to Atlanta.

The city doesn't turn out to be the safe zone the media promised. Atlanta is overrun with zombies that quickly swamp Rick and his horse. The animal is lost, but Rick holds the creatures off with his gun—though the shots only draw more Walkers. A stranger named Glenn comes to Rick's rescue and gets him back out of the city via a rooftop escape.

Glenn tells Rick that the government's plan to herd everyone into the cities was a failure. All it did was provide food for the undead, turning everyone within the city limits into these creatures. Rick collapses when he thinks about what must have happened to his family. Glenn gives him a moment to compose himself before they continue their trek to the camp where Glenn lives. The camp is made up of travelers who had been trying to reach the city but never made it. Rick is elated to discover Lori and Carl are among these survivors.

ISSUE 3

WIDE PANEL: Rick, Lori, and Carl are embracing much like they were on the last page of issue two. We should see Shane again in this panel. He should be standing next to them, putting his hand on Rick's shoulder.

SYNOPSIS: Rick's wife and son aren't the only people from his town to survive. His partner, Shane Walsh, is also in the camp. Shane had convinced Lori to leave home under the impression that the hospital was secured and that Rick would be safe if he came out of his coma. Now that he's reunited with his family, Rick finally allows the enormity of the situation to affect him, and he is filled with a mix of terror and relief.

Shane introduces Rick to the rest of the group of strangers who have found the camp and united to survive. Later, one of those strangers, Dale, warns Rick that Shane's intentions toward Lori do not seem entirely pure. But Rick refuses to even consider the suggestion that his friend would betray him in any way.

While Rick and Shane are off hunting, they come across a Walker tearing into a deer carcass, while back in camp, another rogue creature attacks. Dale decapitates the zombie, but its severed head refuses to die. A finishing shot alerts Rick and Shane to the trouble, and they hurry back to find the situation under control—although nerves are frayed. Lori seeks comfort in her husband's arms while Shane can only look on.

Fairly early on in the series, it began to look as if Robert Kirkman had his first true writing success. But to maintain that success, changes had to be made for the book to proceed. His good friend Moore was unable to keep up with the monthly schedule. After the first six issues came out on an unreliable schedule of irregular release dates, it was clear that the situation needed to be addressed.

"When a comic book is just starting out, if it doesn't come out regularly, people lose interest very quickly," says Kirkman. "Having the string of failures I had before *The Walking Dead*, the last thing I wanted to do when I had my first success was let something derail it. I had a pretty tough conversation with Tony and had to explain to him that I was going to have to take him off the book and find someone else to take over."

Moore stayed on creating covers for the series over the next year and a half and providing supplemental materials for the initial trade paperbacks and covers collection. For interiors beyond issue no. 6, Kirkman contacted Charlie Adlard, an artist he'd worked with when Funk-O-Tron published *Codeflesh*, written by Joe Casey with art by Adlard.

When it came time to find a new artist for *The Walking Dead*, Kirkman knew Adlard's style—and his ability to make deadlines—was exactly what the new series required. "He just e-mailed me out of the blue," Adlard recalls. "The headline of the e-mail was 'Do you want to make money?' He was rather predicting the future, but I don't think he suspected it would be the success that we've had."

ABOVE: Charlie Adlard brought his distinct style, highlighted by a heavier use of black inks, into play from the very first panel of issue no. 7.

Adlard wasn't familiar with *The Walking Dead*, so he quickly read through the first issues to get a handle on the project. "It started as a slow burn," he admits. "I certainly didn't think, 'Well, this is the greatest thing I've ever read.' But I certainly didn't think it was the opposite, either. I thought it was pretty good, so I just carried on and then three or four issues in, it sort of just came to me how good this comic was. By the sixth issue, I was hooked in for the long haul."

"Bringing in Charlie really did set the book on fire, so to speak," Kirkman adds. "Once Charlie came on, we were producing books at a regular clip." The speed differential between Moore and Adlard wasn't the only noticeable difference. The two artists had distinctly different approaches to the page. "Tony is very much inspired by *MAD* Magazine artists like Jack Davis," Kirkman explains. "I wanted *The Walking Dead* to be much grittier and more realistic looking. I think Charlie's art style really suited the stories I wanted to tell much better. Between the speed and the shift in style, I think

Charlie really was one of the main pivot moments that led to the massive success of the book."

The change in artists had its benefit, but not everyone was on board initially. Fans of any series can be resistant to change. Though *The Walking Dead*'s readership was still far from record-breaking, there was no question that they were already deeply invested in the series. "I think it was a problem for the fans," admits Adlard. "If you take over on an established book like *Batman* or *Spider-Man*, you know that character's been around for forty, fifty years plus. The fans are used to change because no one lasts that long on any book. You come in and take over; it's not like this great big twist of style, because people are used to that sort of thing. But on *The Walking Dead*, all the fans were used to six issues of that one look. So coming in and changing it rather radically was quite a thing. It took a lot of people a long time to get used to me."

It wasn't like the comic was suddenly being published in color, but the shift in artwork was fairly dramatic to the trained eye. "Tony and I pretty much are [at] opposite ends of the spectrum in a lot of ways," says Adlard. "Tony dealt a lot more with lines and the detail within the lines. . . . I deal a lot more with mood and atmosphere. And I use a lot more black."

Seeing as how the comic book world is filled with artists who could have mimicked Moore's style, Adlard knew that any concern over these differences had not stopped him from being hired. "Personally, for me, it wasn't an issue coming in and drawing after somebody else," he says. "Because I'm always of the opinion that if somebody calls me up and asks me to draw something for them—because I've got a fairly distinct style—I never think they want me to draw like somebody else. Why get in touch with me if that's the case?"

Although there can be little doubt that the characters are the same whether in the first six issues or beyond, the changes in artwork are noticeable. "I took somebody else's characters, did my own riff on them," Adlard says. "It wasn't a problem for me. I've done that many, many times before. As the book grew and grew, I obviously continued to introduce my own

ABOVE: A study in contrasts of the different approaches Charlie Adlard (left) and Tony Moore (right) took in drawing Rick Grimes.

THE ART OF CHARLIE ADLARD

"Comics, for me, are the most creatively fulfilling thing I could possibly do."
—Charlie Adlard

ABOVE: Charlie Adlard's cover to issue no. 27 (released April 2006) is part of a series of covers from the fifth story arc, with characters clothed in riot gear found in the prison the survivors called home from issues no. 13 through 48.

CONTINUED

ABOVE: The cover to issue no. 79 (released November 2010) is the first in a series of covers in the fourteenth story arc that focus on the zombies. It follows a series of covers in the thirteenth arc in which no zombies appeared on the covers.

ABOVE: The success of *The Walking Dead* has allowed Adlard to create unique pieces for marketing the comic books, like this art of a fan-favorite character he drew for a comic book convention.

CONTINUED ▶

ABOVE: A double-page spread from issue no. 78 reveals that the Walker threat certainly hasn't diminished since issue no. 1.

characters, established my own identity a lot more so I could call the book my own, and I was less and less like the secondary artist sort of thing."

With the transition of artists, Cliff Rathburn was brought in to provide the gray tones (or "coloring") for the series, and later, Rus Wooton took on the lettering responsibilities from Kirkman. As the new creative team settled into a working rhythm, they continued to expand on the action-drama formula that was more focused on drama than action. In terms of the artwork, the dramatic elements of the story were those that Charlie Adlard embraced

ABOVE: Adlard enjoys the challenge of making the scenes where characters simply sit around discussing their situation visually interesting, as he did on page 21 of issue no. 10.

most. "The tricky stuff is drawing interesting, dialogue-heavy scenes," he notes. "That's when it becomes a challenge. The more of a challenge for me, the more interesting it is. I kind of thrive off of those five- or six-page talking-head moments, because it is a challenge to get pages like that interesting."

Adlard looks to Kirkman's written dialogue for inspiration as he illustrates the expressive characters having their deep discussions. After dozens of issues together, Kirkman has fallen into a certain comfort level with the artist, sometimes writing panel descriptions that can be as simple as "Close on Rick" or "Close on Michonne." "Those are the things I really, really enjoy doing," Adlard says. "I really get off on the human emotion more than the chopping up zombies into little bits. On a creative level, anyone can do that sort of stuff. Anyone can do gore. To be able to do the stuff that arguably makes *The Walking Dead* work really well as a comic is the real exciting stuff for me."

The artist isn't the only one who finds that element of the series exciting. *The Walking Dead*'s devoted fan base has grown substantially over the years. "The initial printing of the first issue sold something like seven thousand copies," Stephenson notes. "That was in 2003. Today, we're selling over six times that many copies per issue. There really aren't too many comics that experience that kind of sustained increase in sales, especially over a period as long as eight years."

The success of the series isn't limited to the monthly comic book issues, either. Each arc has been collected into a six-issue trade

***The Walking Dead* Comic Book Series**
Original Six-Issue Arc | "Days Gone Bye"

ISSUE 4

SMALL PANEL: Close on the scene we saw through Glenn's window. Make sure we can see Carl.

SMALL PANEL: Rick is leaning down to talk to Carl. As he does so . . . he's putting his hat on Carl.

SMALL PANEL: Lori is leaning over at Rick looking even angrier.

SYNOPSIS: In light of the recent attack, Rick thinks it's time to move on. Their camp is too close to the Walker-filled city, and winter is coming. But Shane doesn't want to leave. He expects that government representatives will come riding through at any time, and he doesn't want to risk missing them. Rick agrees to stay, but he insists that they need more guns.

Much to Lori's distress, Rick accompanies Glenn on his next trip into Atlanta, going farther into the city than Glenn has ever gone before. To cover their scent, the men coat their bodies with the viscera of the zombie Rick and Shane killed the day before. The disgusting plan works, allowing them to slip into a gun shop and stock up. Rain starts to fall as they head back, and they have to run for it to make it out of the city with their lives and all the guns they can carry.

Back at camp, Shane tries to comfort Lori as she waits for her husband. But Shane is also concerned for himself and the status of his relationship with Lori after an earlier night on the road to Atlanta . . . a night that Lori insists was a mistake.

ISSUE 5

WIDE PANEL: Just a shot of the camp...everyone is depressed, looking down...show as many as you can in the shot. Carl should be making
a face at Sophia...who should be making a face back at him (they are
kids). Just make everyone sort of look like they're reflecting on all
the horrible things they've been talking about.

SYNOPSIS: Everyone at camp is getting better at handling weapons following a couple weeks of gun training. Lori is less than thrilled that Rick has been teaching Carl to shoot, but the seven-year-old is surprisingly skilled with a weapon. Rick allows his son to carry a gun full-time on the condition that he has to be responsible with it.

Donna is upset that Dale is sharing his RV with Andrea and Amy, two young women that are many years his junior. The older man insists that nothing untoward is happening, and Rick shifts the conversation to the cold weather, which Shane takes as a veiled reference to Rick's wanting to move camp. Dale expresses concern at how tightly wound Shane has become.

Sitting around the fire at night, the new friends share their personal tales of what brought them together. Zombies suddenly overrun the camp, sending the serene night into pandemonium. Amy is killed, but her sister is forced to shoot her in the head so she does not reanimate. Carl's gun skills save his mother when she drops her weapon. And Jim is bitten. He doesn't immediately die, but he is still doomed.

ISSUE 6

SMALL PANEL: Close on Shane... still pointing the gun at Rick.

SMALL PANEL: Rick is crying... yeah... again... his hands are up... he's pleading with Shane.

SYNOPSIS: It's the morning after the camp was overrun. Amy has been buried. Jim is nursing his wound. But the underlying tension boils over when Carl makes an innocent comment about how they'll need less food now, and Shane snaps at Rick.

Dale tries to comfort Andrea, while Donna attempts to make the last hours of Jim's life more manageable. Jim asks to be left at the edge of Atlanta and allowed to turn so that maybe he can reunite in death with the family that he left behind when he fled the city.

The next morning, Rick wants to go hunting with Shane alone so they can discuss the situation, but Shane is tired of talking and lashes out in anger. Lori defends her husband, leaving scratches across Shane's face, as the rest of the camp freezes in shock. Shane storms off into the woods, and Rick gives chase, hoping to reason with his friend.

Shane screams at Rick, blaming him for returning, for being alive at all. If only Rick hadn't shown up, everything would be fine with Shane and Lori. Shane turns his gun on Rick. He's about to fire, but a bullet pierces his neck, killing him. Carl acted to protect his father, but the child can't understand why Shane isn't getting back up like the zombies do.

paperback and, later, twelve-issue hardbacks, twenty-four-issue omnibuses, and, ultimately, a forty-eight-issue compendium. There has also been a collected volume of the comic book covers, and Image started rerunning the series in weekly rereleases of the original issues.

ABOVE: The cover to *The Walking Dead Volume 2* trade paperback, containing issues 7–12, released November 2004, with cover art by Tony Moore. When all the trade paperback covers are lined up side by side, the zombies continue in an unending line of walking dead.

OPPOSITE: *The Walking Dead* issue no. 6 was released in March 2004. This was the last issue for which Tony Moore provided interior art, but he continued to draw the series' covers until issue no. 24.

PREVIOUS SPREAD: Tony Moore's original sketch and final art for the cover of the first trade paperback collection, *Days Gone Bye*.

Over the course of his time at Image Comics, Robert Kirkman became such an integral part of the team that he was invited to join the company's four remaining original partners in 2008. Kirkman eventually developed his own imprint, Skybound Entertainment, under the Image banner, allowing him a greater ability to work in the medium that will always be his first love.

Although he is now an executive producer and writer on the TV series based on his source material, he has no intention of giving up the comic book life. "I love working in comics," Kirkman proclaims. "I plan on continuing to work in comics for the rest of my life. Despite all the other stuff I do, if you asked me what I did for a living, I'd still say I was a comic book writer. Even though I could say that I was a TV writer and my mom will be more impressed, I don't really care. I know that I'm going to be known as *The Walking Dead* guy for the rest of my life. It's going to be very hard to do something to top *The Walking Dead*. At the same time, I want to at least try to do different projects. To be honest, I really have enjoyed working in television. I have other ideas for shows. It would be nice to eventually do another show that's not *The Walking Dead*. Maybe I'll be lucky enough to do that someday. And then at some point, maybe I'll retire. But we'll see."

TWO

FROM PAGE TO SCREEN:

DEVELOPING *THE WALKING DEAD* FOR TELEVISION

As sales of *The Walking Dead* comic books and collected editions increased, Hollywood started calling. Robert Kirkman was fielding offers to adapt his work for the screen from a variety of noted directors, screenwriters, and other production entities. "It was always stuff that I wasn't really into," he recalls. "They wanted to turn it into an action movie. They wanted to incorporate super-zombies. There were different aspects to *The Walking Dead* that they just didn't seem to get." The early success of the comic book allowed Kirkman to be a bit more selective about whom he wanted to partner with in realizing his vision on-screen.

The comic was starting to provide him and Charlie Adlard with comfortable enough incomes that they didn't have to accept the first offer that came their way. Luckily, Academy Award–nominated multi-hyphenate (producer-director-screenwriter) Frank Darabont was about to take a trip to his local comic book store.

"It was something I literally came across at House of Secrets comic book shop in Burbank," Darabont recalls of his first glimpse of the comic book not previously on his radar. "I was just browsing. I had not heard of Kirkman. I had not heard of this comic book. I walked in, and I saw the first trade paperback on the shelf there. I was immediately drawn to it, because it's zombies. Right up my alley."

Darabont, a fan of the zombie genre for years, read the six-issue trade paperback straight through that night and was on the phone with his agent the next day asking to look into the rights. It was exactly the concept he'd been looking for to develop a long-form exploration of zombies. Calls were made and contacts forwarded. Suddenly Kirkman found himself on

ABOVE: Released in January 2006, issue no. 25 (left) is the first of *The Walking Dead* covers drawn by Charlie Adlard. More than forty-eight issues later, the TV series premiered around the release of issue no. 78, in October 2010 (right).

PREVIOUS SPREAD: The television production would look to the comic book for inspiration whenever possible, often re-creating images directly for the screen and for the marketing of the series.

the phone with someone who was saying all the things he'd been waiting to hear.

"Frank kind of came out of nowhere," Kirkman says. "He called me up and was like, 'Oh, by the way, I'm the man who wrote and directed *The Shawshank Redemption*. I usually do dramatic movies, but now I want to do this zombie show. And I want to make it a character study where the zombies are just a backdrop.' He knew exactly what to tell me, and his body of work spoke for itself. So, I knew that he was the right guy pretty much immediately."

According to Kirkman, Darabont's call came a little more than two years into the series, around the release of issue no. 25 in early 2006. In the comic, Rick Grimes and the remaining group of survivors had settled into a new home that would keep them relatively protected for the next two-dozen issues. But had Kirkman himself found the right home for his comic? Even with a producer of Darabont's caliber, the series was not guaranteed to get a green light. It wouldn't be until issue no. 78, almost five years later, that the series premiered on AMC.

Hollywood executives scour the bestseller lists for books and comics and other source material to adapt, but that's not what motivated Darabont to take *The Walking Dead* off the shelf. Darabont explains, "Ultimately what I found most intriguing about this project—specifically, Kirkman's *The Walking Dead*—was the intensely character-driven approach that he had taken. I thought this would be a really great, adult way of getting into the zombie sandbox and telling this kind of story in a highly serialized, long-term manner, which really has never been done."

Darabont has always been a fan of survival tales, citing *Lord of the Flies* and the works of Stephen King as some of his greatest inspirations. It's understandable that the producer would be quick to note King's writing, as Darabont has adapted three of the author's works for film: *The Mist, The Green Mile*, and *The Shawshank Redemption*.

Many of the projects that had been an influence on Darabont were a product of the decades he'd lived through. "When I was growing up during the Cold War, there were plenty of apocalyptic scenarios being drawn," he notes. "Certainly under the threat of nuclear holocaust, which was very keen at that time. Science fiction would delve into those areas very frequently, and some of my favorite films are drawn from that tradition, whether it's the original *Planet of the Apes* or a novel like *No Blade of Grass*. It's a fascinating pressure cooker in which to put a group of characters and then see what happens."

Darabont started taking the idea around to the networks, ending up at NBC, where he was asked to submit a pilot script. As Darabont got to work on the adaptation, Kirkman did his best not to get too excited over the idea of his work moving to the small screen. "I was told that it was pretty much a lock for them to shoot a pilot just because of Frank's standing in the industry," Kirkman recalls. "It would be crazy for them to turn down a pilot written by Frank Darabont that he was going to direct. But they ended up coming back after Frank had written the draft, and I believe the exact quote was 'This is really great. Does there have to be zombies in it?' From that point, it kind of fell apart."

Just because NBC lost interest, however, didn't mean the project was dead. Darabont now had a pilot script to shop, and he took it every place he could. Unfortunately, the reception was very much the same as it had been with NBC. "I would list the networks that turned it down, but I don't have to," Kirkman admits. "Because it was pretty much all of them. It just kind of went into a drawer for awhile."

Still, like the zombies that inspired the work, the pilot would rise again five years later. All it took was some time, a new partner, and a massive shift in pop-culture interest in the subject matter. "In [those] five years, grandmas started walking into bookstores and buying zombie joke books for their [grand]kids," Darabont says. "There's zombie puppets. It's crazy how it's become this cultural wave of things." Darabont believes that all the interest harkens back to what made zombies such a fascinating subject for Kirkman: George Romero's *Night of the Living Dead*.

Even with the renewed interest in the subject matter, one key component was still necessary to bring life to *The Walking Dead*. Darabont was close to tapping out on the project when his friend Gale Anne Hurd, a veteran film and TV producer, approached him with an offer to team up on the project. "I've known Gale for years," Darabont says. "I think the world of her. She's a formidable producer and a gracious, fantastic friend. I should partner up with her more, clearly, because the first place she took it to was AMC, and they said yes immediately. So I have Gale to thank. We all do—if you dig the show, you have Gale Anne Hurd to thank for the fact that this thing exists."

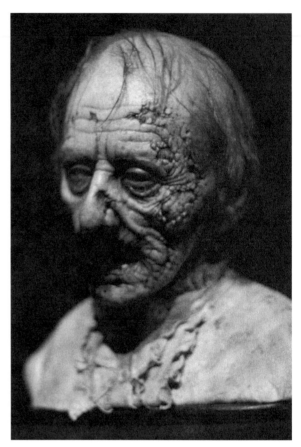

ABOVE: The pilot script wasn't the only thing Frank Darabont took with him when he was shopping his pitch for *The Walking Dead*. To help fully realize his vision, he contacted a friend, special effects makeup designer Greg Nicotero, to assist with the visual aids for his meetings. Together, with his team at KNB EFX, Nicotero worked with Darabont to figure out how to create zombies with a look that neither of them had seen before. To make sure that the presentation was compelling and visually exciting, Nicotero constructed a couple of zombie busts and other supplemental material that Darabont could show the networks.

OPPOSITE: The first page of Kirkman and Moore's revised proposal for *The Walking Dead* comic book, which directly references the oft-imitated television broadcasts from *Night of the Living Dead*.

Like Kirkman and Darabont, Hurd was a fan of the zombie genre that evolved from Romero's work. As someone who began her career working with Roger Corman on his classic movies and straight-up horror/exploitation

GEORGE ROMERO'S
NIGHT OF THE LIVING DEAD

"I like my zombies served up Romero-style." —Frank Darabont

ABOVE: The *Night of the Living Dead* UK theatrical poster emphasized sexuality over violence, though the actual film was notable for its controversial depiction of gore.

When speaking with anyone involved with *The Walking Dead* comic books or TV series, the conversation eventually turns to the so-called "Godfather of the Zombie," George Romero. The filmmaker and his cowriter John Russo are credited with redefining the zombie for modern audiences when they produced the cult-classic horror movie *Night of the Living Dead* in 1968.

Prior to the release of the film, what little zombie lore there was had grown out of the mystical voodoo practices of Haiti. The original zombie was a corpse placed under a spell to reanimate its body. The creature had no will of its own and existed only to serve the commands of its master. It did not seek out human flesh, nor could it create more zombies, as we have come to know them today, thanks to Romero.

The filmmaker himself was inspired by Richard Matheson's 1954 book *I Am Legend*, which centered on a worldwide apocalypse brought about by a disease that created vampire-like creatures. Romero's film, *Night of the Living Dead*, follows a group of strangers in rural Pennsylvania who find themselves trapped in a farmhouse under attack by undead ghouls. All along the eastern seaboard, the recently deceased are coming back to life to consume the flesh of the living. No one knows for certain the cause of the outbreak, but it has been determined that a bullet to the brain or a strong blow to the head will stop the creatures.

Many critics bashed the film for the way it sensationalized violence and for its heavy reliance on gore. But some praised it as groundbreaking in the horror genre—which indeed it was. The film captured the imaginations of many of the people who would become involved in *The Walking Dead*, and the rules established in the film are the cornerstone for the world of Kirkman's creation, as well as for much of the current zombie subset in film and literature.

ABOVE: The shuffling zombies recently risen from the dead gave birth to a new kind of movie monster that inspired a pop-culture trend in zombie stories decades later.

films, she too was immediately attracted to *The Walking Dead* comics. And though one might not think that AMC would be the right fit, the subject matter turned out to be exactly what they were seeking for their development slate.

Executive Producer David Alpert is quick to point out why the network of *Mad Men* and *Breaking Bad* wasn't an entirely unlikely partner: "You look at AMC and you don't necessarily think *The Walking Dead*, but they have a huge fan base with Fearfest every Halloween. The classic horror movie marathon gets some of the highest ratings on the network. And that was sort of interesting. But the thing that ultimately made them the right home was the fact that they let characters and stories breathe. They let the stories take their time."

Kirkman agrees that the network was the perfect home for his work. "I think AMC will be known as a visionary network when people look back on this time," he says. "They were the only network that would say, 'Yeah, okay. Zombies. That's something we can do.' But every other network didn't want to even consider it, just because of the subject matter and the kind of things that you have to do in a zombie story. AMC—even from the get-go—was very willing to take those risks."

Rather than simply committing to producing a pilot and then testing that single episode, as is traditional in television development, AMC ordered six episodes based on the strength of

the pilot script. To Darabont, this was a very pleasant surprise. "All too often you get one shot at it," he says. "You get to make a pilot, and then somebody decides whether they're even going to air it or not. A lot of pilots that are made don't even get aired; don't even get that chance. And then there's the factor that follows that, which is your pilot does air, but you don't get a chance with the audience. You get one shot at it. Here, we got to make six episodes that had the opportunity to find an audience, to enlist the viewers. I think there's tremendous wisdom in that."

Joel Stillerman, senior vice president of original programming, production & digital content, explains the network's decision to commit to more than just the pilot: "First, we knew we had something that had not been done before. There is a lot of pressure in that, but there is also great opportunity. We knew we had a great team, and we had total confidence in the quality of the comics as source material. If we didn't have the comics as a road map, it would have been a much harder decision."

"We also had a healthy interest in the genre, well-executed, in series form," adds Charlie Collier, president of AMC. "Notwithstanding the long history of zombies as a popular film genre, a zombie series was something we had never seen on television before. That uniqueness always interests us."

AMC did not simply buy the initial pilot outright, though. The network was developing a reputation for character-driven, deliberately paced dramas. While Darabont's pilot script met many of the criteria the network was looking

OPPOSITE: Issue no. 3, page 6 is an example of one of the earlier pages in the comic series that allows the action–and the dialogue–to pause for a scene of quiet reflection.

EPISODE I: "DAYS GONE BYE"

Teleplay by Frank Darabont
Directed by Frank Darabont

RICK: I woke up today. In the hospital. Came home. That's all I know.

MORGAN: But you know about the dead people, right?

RICK: Yeah, I saw a lot of that. Out on the loading docks. Piled in trucks.

MORGAN: No, not the ones they put down. The ones they didn't. The Walkers.

SYNOPSIS: Sheriff's Deputy Rick Grimes pulls his police cruiser to the side of a desolate road where abandoned tents, forgotten trash, and fly-ridden bodies sit dead in their cars, surrounding a gas station with nothing to offer the cruiser's empty tank.

Rick is about to give up on the station when a noise suggests he is not alone. Beneath the cars, he sees the shuffling feet of a little girl in bunny slippers. Rick offers the girl help, but when she turns, he sees that her face is half eaten away. He cannot save her in life, but he can offer her final death. Rick shoots the girl in the head, saving himself and ending her misery.

Flashback to another time: Rick opens up to his partner, Shane, about the problems in his marriage. He's concerned about a recent argument he had with his wife, Lori, in front of their son. The conversation is interrupted when a call for backup comes in from the state police. Rick and Shane race off to intercept suspects in a high-speed chase. During the melee, Rick is shot through the chest and everything goes white.

CONTINUED

Rick slowly regains consciousness in the hospital, but no one answers his calls for help. The place is empty, except for a lone, mangled body in the hall. Bullet holes riddle the walls above pools of blood. A chained set of doors holds an ominous warning scrawled in paint: DON'T OPEN DEAD INSIDE.

The doors slowly move outward, pressing against the chains. Deathly white hands slip through the crack, reaching out. Rick flees the hospital to see rows and rows of dead, decaying bodies outside and the remains of a military camp. He finds a bike on the road and is shocked to see a nearby dead woman come to life. She is decayed beyond recognition with her lower body missing, but she still reaches for Rick.

Rick hurries home to find it abandoned. As he goes back onto the street, someone hits him on the head with a shovel. Rick wakes to find himself in his neighbor's home, tied to the bed by a squatter named Morgan Jones and his son, Duane. They bring Rick up to speed on what happened to the world while he was in his coma and how the undead Walkers now roam the streets.

Duane is despondent when he sees his Walker mother out the window. She died very recently, but Morgan didn't have it in him to kill her before she turned, by the only means that works: destroying the brain.

Rick hopes his own wife and son are alive because they packed clothing and family photos when they left their house. Morgan tells him about the refugee center in Atlanta, and Rick decides to go there to seek out his family, but first he needs a car and some weapons.

Rick, Morgan, and Duane shower and stock up at the sheriff's station, but Morgan isn't ready to leave town yet. Rick gives him a radio so they can communicate when Morgan comes looking for him. As they are about to part, they see a Walker coming up on the other side of the fence. It's Rick's former coworker, Leon. Rick fires a bullet into Leon's head, and the men part ways before other Walkers can be drawn to the noise.

Morgan returns to their temporary home, telling Duane to stay downstairs. He chooses a picture of his wife from happier times, tapes it to the window, and aims his gun on the Walkers in the street below. He fires on a couple of them and waits for the noise to draw others. When he sees his wife, he struggles to pull the trigger. With tears in his eyes, he takes aim again, but he just can't do it.

CONTINUED

Rick has no such problem with the stranger he saw the day before. He stops on his way out of town to fire a shot into the head of the woman missing half her body, putting the creature out of her misery. With that settled, he drives down abandoned roads, calling out for anyone that can hear him on the radio.

His voice is picked up at a camp outside Atlanta, but they can't answer back. Officer Shane Walsh takes up the CB, unaware that he's calling out to his friend. He's there with Rick's wife and son, Carl. Lori and Shane argue over her plan to put signs on the highway to warn people away from the city, resolving their discussion with a secret kiss.

In the present time, Rick has abandoned his cruiser and found a farmhouse with dead inside. The sole survivor is a horse that Rick takes to continue his journey into Atlanta.

The city seems abandoned, but it's not. A helicopter flies overhead, but when Rick goes after it, he stumbles upon a street filled with Walkers. They take down the horse, but Rick finds refuge in an abandoned tank. As Rick contemplates his options, trapped inside the vehicle with his gun bag out on the street, a voice on the radio breaks through.

ABOVE: Series Producer-Director-Writer Frank Darabont lines up a shot from the tank's-eye view of the zombie-filled streets of downtown Atlanta.

for, they requested a revision to make it a bit less event-driven and focus even more on the characters. "That was made very clear to us from our very first meeting when we brought the project into AMC," Hurd explains. "They said, 'Our shows allow time for the characters and the world to breathe. This is not a series where there has to be quick cutting, where we have to get on with plot, plot, plot. We really want to carve out time to be with the characters.'"

In a world where the technology exists to seamlessly remove pauses in actors' dialogue, Darabont was writing for a faster pace. The request to slow down the action opened up the storytelling for him. "I literally took that pilot script—that first script that I wrote—and split

it, narratively speaking, right down the middle," he explains. "I split it in two and then expanded each half of that into its own episode." This gave him the leisure to "put on his character hat," as he calls it, and really dig into the different roles in the manner he was accustomed to with his film work.

The other benefit of slowing the pace, beyond matching AMC's sensibilities, was that it really fit the source material. Kirkman packed a lot into the first six issues of *The Walking Dead*. Even with so much focus on the Walkers in these issues, the series as a whole became far more about the human interaction. The difference between a twenty-two-page comic book script and a fifty-page TV episode script is more

The definitive moment in the opening issue of *The Walking Dead* comic book occurs on the final page, when Rick fires on the Walker torso. Robert Kirkman explains the importance of the zombie character and its impact on the story: "In the comic book series, that moment was meant to make a statement. It says a lot about Rick that he has his encounter with the bicycle zombie when he comes out of the hospital, and he's just horrified by what he is seeing. [Later,] he's got to go get his wife and he's in his police car and he takes the time to go back to that zombie and put her out of her misery. Without even really doing any dialogue, that tells you the kind of person that Rick Grimes is,

ABOVE, TOP: Rick Grimes finds more than just a mode of transportation along the side of the road.

ABOVE, BOTTOM: Frank Darabont works with Andrew Lincoln and Melissa Cowan in setting up the scene in which Rick ends the zombie's suffering.

OPPOSITE: Issue no. 1, page 10 shows Rick's initial reaction to the half-missing body in comic form. Translating this scene and his subsequent return at the end of issue no. 1 were pivotal moments in the pilot episode.

and hopefully it gets you invested in the character and makes you want to come back and read more stories about the guy."

In the pilot episode, Frank Darabont took what existed on the comic page and expanded it not only to make a statement about Rick Grimes, but also provide

CONTINUED

commentary on Morgan Jones. Morgan and his son, Duane, appear in the first issue of the comic book and then disappear for a while. They make a brief appearance in a short story in the Image Comics Holiday Special in 2005, but it was not until their return in issue no. 58 that the readers discovered their fate. This presented Darabont with an opening to explore.

Kirkman looks at that moment with good-natured chagrin. "I have Morgan casually mention that his wife died. I think I even implied that she was a zombie, but we don't really delve into it very much. Frank took that nugget and said, 'Silly Kirkman, why did you move off that so quickly? You should have delved into that and made it much more of a key moment in the series.'"

ABOVE: Morgan pauses just before he aborts his attempt to end his wife's misery.

In the pilot, Morgan leaves his son downstairs and goes up to look through the family photos his wife had packed. He tapes a picture of her in happier times to the window and starts firing on the zombies in the street below. The sound upsets Duane, but it works in drawing more Walkers to the street, including Morgan's wife. Even though Morgan can take out zombie after zombie, he cannot bring himself to shoot his wife when he has the gun trained on her.

The moment is interspersed with the scene of Rick firing a shot in the head of the legless zombie. Since the sheriff's deputy doesn't have any relationship with the character beyond the pity he feels for her, it's an easier situation for him than what Morgan is experiencing, but it still says a lot about each character and the TV series as a whole. "I think what Frank was able to do in the pilot really enhanced that scene and pulled much more emotion out of it," Kirkman says. "It really heightened everything. The best moments in the show for me are when I can see Frank and the other writers take something from the comic book and enhance it to the point where it embarrasses me."

The juxtaposition of scenes brought a level of depth to the series that made it stand out from a traditional zombie story as a character study of the living. "That was the whole purpose," Gale Anne Hurd explains. "To contrast the way that different people who are surviving in this world handle the challenges. Morgan can't move on with his life. He can't shoot his wife, even though she's become a zombie. Even though he knows he's not going to get her back in the way that she was before. In fact, if she were to get close to him or his son, she would try to devour them. But it's something that, try as he might, he cannot pull the trigger. If he can't pull the trigger, he can't leave. And he grapples with it every day.

But Rick has to move on. Even though he's not sure that his wife and son have survived, he has hope, since they clearly got out of town because the family photo albums are gone."

It was not just the writing on the page that made that moment work. Makeup effects have come a long way since the days of *Night of the Living Dead*. It really sold the moment to be able to combine a human actor with makeup and visual effects to create the character that became known as "bicycle girl."

The character was devised to elicit sympathy from the audience, not horror. To achieve this required the technical challenge of being mobile while missing half her body, but still having an expressive face that could convey the emotion of the scene. It was not something that a puppet could perform. It took the work of Key Special Effects Makeup Supervisor Greg Nicotero of KNB EFX Group and the visual effects team at Stargate Studios to bring the character to life. "That was a great blending between prosthetic makeup and visual effects," says Visual Effects Supervisor Jason Sperling. "What Greg was able to do

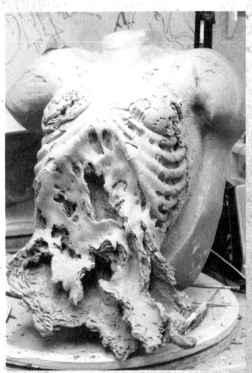

ABOVE, TOP: An early design sketch for the character that would become known as "bicycle girl."

ABOVE, BOTTOM: A bicycle girl torso piece created from a mold of the actress's body.

CONTINUED

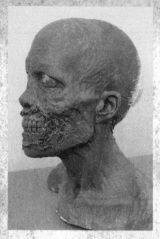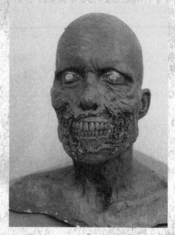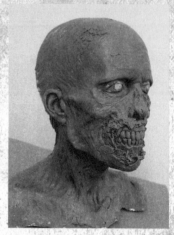

with his work on set was to make up this amazingly beautiful woman, who when put through Greg's eye, gets turned into an incredibly dramatic figure."

Nicotero flew the Atlanta-based actress out to his studio in Los Angeles. There, the makeup effects team molded a face and body cast of her to create both a front and back piece that would fit around her upper body. "We ended up sculpting the torso section," Nicotero explains. "All the internal organs had fallen out, so we had all this skin that was sort of draped down." The complete makeup incorporated six or seven distinct pieces that were applied to the actress through a three-hour makeup process on the day of filming when they were back on location.

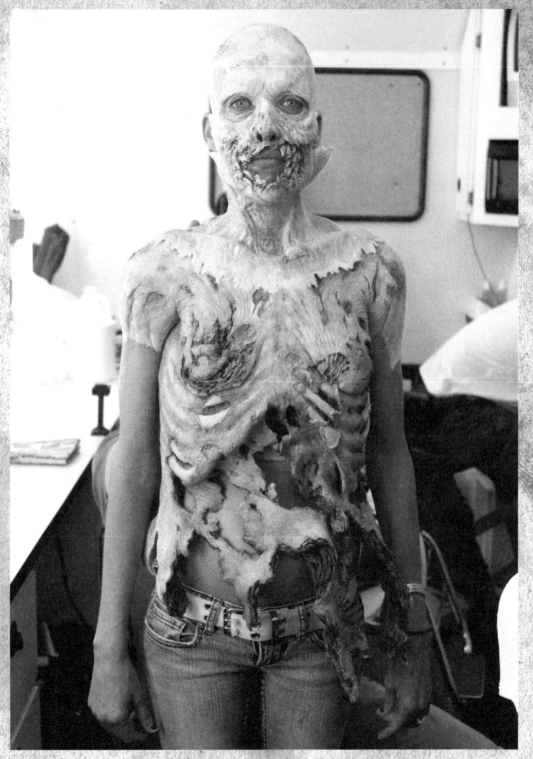

ABOVE: Midway through the makeup process on the day of filming.

OPPOSITE: The final element of the bicycle girl costume was a pair of blue leggings that would allow her lower body to be digitally removed in postproduction.

CONTINUED

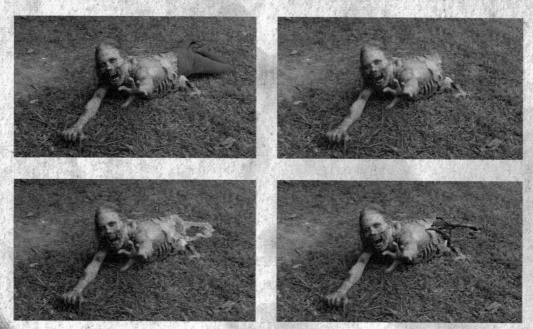

ABOVE: After the visual effects artists removed the blue leggings, they added each trailing bit of her body digitally, incorporating a prop femur bone provided by the makeup team.

The team mocked up dentures that were put on her life cast, and then sculpted the clay around it so that the teeth were always exposed. "This character was supposed to be partially sympathetic. She wasn't a monster, but she was supposed to just look kind of creepy," Nicotero says. "By angling the brows downward a little bit, in the sculpture, it actually made her a little more sad looking. It makes a big difference." The sculpture, done by makeup artist Jeremy Aiello, made it appear as if the nose was drooping down off her face to add to the sorrowful expression.

Makeup covered the top half of the actress's body, but her lower section still had to be removed and replaced by visual effects. On the day of filming, she wore a pair of blue leggings that could be keyed out in postproduction so the effects team would be able to add in their 3-D geometry. "Our major challenge on that was really to blend where Greg's work ended and where ours began," explains Sperling. "That seam point in the torso area was our main point of focus."

Nicotero provided the visual effects artists with a femur bone and some other torso parts they could use to texture the 3-D geometry and seamlessly blend bicycle girl together. But it wasn't just adding details that provided the challenge. "The tough part about a shot like that, where you're going to do any kind of a body removal, is when you see into the cavity," explains Stargate Studios CEO and Visual Effects Supervisor Sam Nicholson. "A lot of credit goes to our 3-D team that completely modeled all of her insides: her intestines, her spine, the bones that are hanging out, the flesh. They exactly match the textures of Greg's work."

To do this kind of matching requires extensive photo coverage of the finished makeup on the day of filming. "Then, we texture-wrapped that exact texture onto the 3-D model so that it's like wallpaper, but it's flesh," says Nicholson. "And you sculpt this around the 3-D parts, and then they have to be animated so that they move around right in the grass. If you really look at it, it really looks like an intestine dragging across the grass. And then the grass has to be painted through. Because obviously, where she's blue, it punches a hole in it—there's nothing behind it. So then you have to shoot other grass, and that grass has to be textured to look like it's been crushed and she's been dragging through it."

The entire process went through almost forty revisions that had to be done very quickly, with Darabont apprised at every possible stage of development. The overriding question the team had to ask was if they had gone too far into the decay. "We didn't want to distract from her face," Nicholson says, remembering the true focus of the scene. "We wanted it to be real, but we didn't want your eye to just go to the guts." In the end, they created a standout look that lent strength to one of the more memorable scenes in the first season.

ABOVE: The end result of bicycle girl in full makeup became a key part of the episode and the marketing campaign for the series.

"BICYCLE GIRL" STORYBOARDS

THE WALKING DEAD
EPISODE 1 PAN 1

PAGE:
4-2-10

STOP

START

22/6

RICK'S P.O.V.
TILT UP FROM BIKE
HELMET TO FALLEN
BIKE.
FOLLOW BLOOD STAINS
TO TORSO GIRL ...

3 & 4 - PAN WITH RICK AS HE CROSSES FRAME TO UNDER THE TREE.

RICK LIFTS HIS HAT UP OUT OF HIS EYES.

HE SQUATS DOWN TILT-DOWN TO FOLLOW

CAMERA TRACKS WITH TORSO GIRL AS SHE INCHES THROUGH FRAME.
☆ NOTE:
CAMERA KEEPS ABOVE HER WAIST.

- RICK SITS, WATCHING THE TORSO GIRL CRAWL THROUGH FRAME.

RICK'S P.O.V.

- WATCHING TORSO-GIRL INCH ALONG...

- IT'S PAINFUL TO WATCH...

- ON RICK -

WATCHING,...

- REACTING...

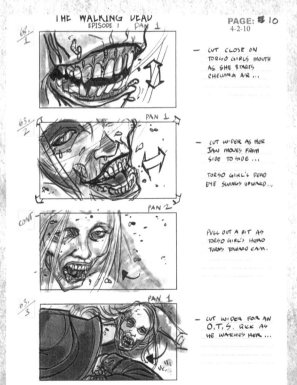

- CUT CLOSE ON TORSO GIRLS MOUTH AS SHE STARTS CHEWING AIR...

- CUT WIDER AS HER JAW MOVES FROM SIDE TO SIDE...

TORSO GIRL'S DEAD EYE SWINGS UPWARD...

PULL OUT A BIT AS TORSO GIRL'S HEAD TURNS TOWARD CAM.

- CUT WIDER FOR AN O.T.S. RICK AS HE WATCHES HER...

① RICK SAD...

RICK:
I'm sorry this happened to you...

② TILT DOWN TO SEE RICK BRING UP HIS PISTOL...

CUT WIDE FOR GUNSHOT,..
TORSO GIRL SLUMPS TO THE GROUND...

HUGE KA-BOOM!
ECHOES LOUDLY. CROWS EXPLODE FROM TREE AND RACE IN EVERY DIRECTION.

- RICK STANDS OVER TORSO GIRL AS HE HOLSTERS HIS WEAPON...

RICK WALKS OFF...

than just numbers. Moving to the slower pace of the television format, the series better reflected the horrors its characters faced.

"*The Walking Dead* isn't a 'run from zombies and hide and shoot Uzis and jump from the buildings and hack zombies' heads off' kind of show," Kirkman is quick to note. "It's all about building tension. That's what Frank was able to do in spades, particularly in the pilot. The pilot has tons of silences and very slow scenes that really inform you as to what this world is like. You see them cruising through downtown Atlanta, walking at a slow pace on that horse, and you hear the silence of the city, which is just absolutely bizarre. You don't ever see a city setting that silent. It really makes the show that much more unique and really informs the viewers as to exactly what kind of ride they're in for. It's really great."

Not only did the producers secure a six-episode order, but AMC agreed to allow them even more time to breathe with an extended first episode that ran for ninety minutes (with limited commercial interruption). But just because the scenes on-screen were slow and deliberate did not mean it was like that behind the cameras. The first episode was shot in fifteen days, which is slightly shorter than usual for a pilot episode, according to Darabont. But that was not a problem for the producer at all. "I actually really love moving at that pace now," he says. "I know, earlier in my career, I had a reputation for moving slowly. I look forward to the day when I have the material and the luxury of moving slowly again. But not every piece of material requires moving slowly. It's not

all brain surgery. It's all surgery, but it's not all brain surgery."

One of the benefits to an extensive résumé, Darabont feels, is that he has reached the point as a director where he doesn't need to think too much about certain scenes. "You don't have to second-guess your decision," he says. "You don't have to do calculus in order to know that the pieces are going to fit together. It's not always a chess game. Sometimes it can be a really fast game of checkers. This was faster than checkers. . . . This was like playing pinball. *Ding ding ding ding!* You see that ball bouncing around, and so you just keep hitting the damn thing. That's what shooting at this pace is, and it's really, really fun."

The pilot laid the groundwork for a series of episodes that would be steeped in the story line set up by Kirkman while taking detours along the way to explore other storytelling options. "We will diverge from that path and gather other cool ideas into it as we go," Darabont states. "But we'll always be following that narrative path that he's laid out. It's a very good one."

Kirkman not only serves as an executive producer on the project, but also as one of the writers. In both roles, he supports Darabont's vision for the adaptation and is often the loudest voice for change in the writers' room, looking forward to the chance to explore new stories with the familiar characters. As this was his first experience writing for television, Kirkman quickly learned how different it is to be in a room full of writers, as opposed to being the lone scribe on his comic series.

"I like to think that writing comics is

ABOVE: Robert Kirkman playfully poses with some of the featured Walkers from the series.

writing without a net, and writing TV is writing with a safety net," he says. "When I'm writing the comics, I'm completely by myself, and I write very quickly. I have my plot, and I know where I'm going, and I know what the characters need to do and where they need to go and everything. But for the most part, I sit down and I go, 'Okay, well this guy's going to die.' And then I kill that guy, cut that guy, and then I move on to the next page."

In television, the plotting for the individual episodes and the future arcs is done in the writers' room, with all of the writing team present. Every suggestion is met with debate and a full exploration of what the idea brings to the story. If a character is going to have his hand cut off, for instance, they consider what it means down the line for that character and the practical applications of going through future plotlines with only one hand. "You pick the scene apart and look at every single angle and every single repercussion, and you work all that stuff out," Kirkman explains. "At the end of the day you

go, 'Well, did that idea pass the test? Is everyone in agreement on that? Should we definitely do that?' It's really a bizarre, democratic, kind of a cool process."

Writing both the comic book and the TV series allows Kirkman to play in two different worlds. Not just because the story lines diverge at points, but because the story has naturally evolved over the course of several years of issues. "I'm so far ahead of the show," Kirkman says, "the cast is almost completely different because so many characters have died. The characters that are living have been through so much that they're almost completely different characters at this point. They behave differently and speak differently."

The TV series allows Kirkman to go back and write again for characters he hasn't worked with in years. "I get to come back and visit old friends that I've murdered, I like to say. And also look at stories I've told from a different perspective and tweak them. I get to do new stuff, because the show does have different characters and different scenes and a lot of things that aren't in the comic book. It really is like going into an alternate dimension and doing a different kind of *Walking Dead*, but it's really a lot of fun."

THREE

BREATHING LIFE INTO THE DEAD

The Walking Dead is a zombie apocalypse tale where the zombies provide the backdrop for an exploration of the human drama. But even as background characters, the entire concept of the series hinges on these creatures. To sell the idea of *The Walking Dead*, the actual walking dead needed to be poignant and terrifying— but, above all, convincing. No matter how powerful the scripts or impressive the production values, if the zombies didn't work, the entire concept would fall apart.

Frank Darabont did not need to look very far to find the right makeup effects company to handle the task. KNB EFX Group has been in the business of special-effects makeup creations for twenty years. They have worked on projects such as *Sin City, Serenity, Kill Bill (Vols. 1 & 2), From Dusk Till Dawn,* and the *Chronicles of Narnia* film series. And it just so happened that the company was cofounded by Greg Nicotero, one of Darabont's closest friends.

Comparing the crew lists of Darabont's productions, one will find many repeated names. Darabont has a team of production people and actors with whom he regularly works because they are experts in their fields and, quite simply, enjoyable to be around. "It's fun to work with your friends," says Darabont. "It's even more fun to work with your geek friends. It's tremendous fun to work with your geek friends when they're as renowned and talented as Greg Nicotero. We've known each other at least twenty years now, so we speak a common language. We've always wanted to do monsters together. We've always certainly wanted to do zombies together. So Greg's having a field day here."

Nicotero echoes the sentiment, counting Darabont among his closest friends. In fact, the entire production team is pretty tight, in part because they have many of the same interests. "We have a shared experience," Nicotero adds. "We all had the same diet of *Famous Monsters* magazine and Ray Harryhausen movies and *Night of the Living Dead* and John Carpenter and *Jaws.* We all sort of fell in love with the same movies."

"My instructions to him when this whole thing began were 'Just do the coolest zombies you can,'" Darabont recalls. "'Bring your *A* game.' And indeed he has, with his company, KNB, and Jake [Garber] and Andy

[Schoneberg] and the folks who work with him. It's so great to have these really world-class makeup effects artists pulling out the stops and having fun surprising us on the set. Every once in a while, they'll sense there's potential for really featuring a zombie in a sequence and will come up with some amazing design work and execute it, and it just shows up on the day. That's really been tremendously fun and rewarding for me."

It helped that the company had experience in the zombie genre on which they could build for a weekly TV series. "We'd done a couple

ABOVE: KNB EFX artist Joe Giles was one of several people who provided their bodies as blank canvases for the makeup team to develop the look of the zombies for the TV series.

PREVIOUS SPREAD: Frank Darabont was so pleased with the final look of the makeup on Giles that the director made him a featured zombie in the pilot episode.

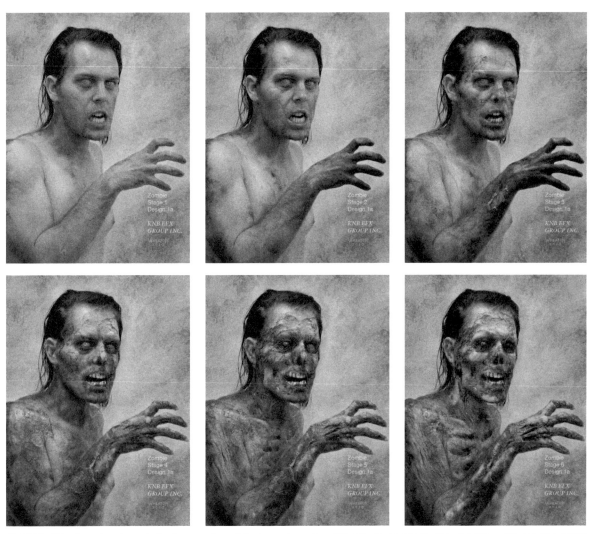

ABOVE: Nicotero developed six stages of zombie decay based on Giles's photo. Under Darabont's guidance, the artist settled on stage-three decay for the pilot, leaving room for the zombies to further decompose as the series continues.

other zombie movies," Nicotero explains. "So we started refining what we felt the zombies could look like, taking into consideration all the other zombie projects that had been made. Some projects, the zombies are running around so fast you never really feature them. We were living much more in the George Romero universe, where they are slow moving when not provoked, but when they're provoked, they can become agitated enough that there's a genuine threat there."

The initial conversations between Nicotero and Darabont centered on the basic question of how long ago the outbreak had occurred, so the makeup effects artists would know how far to go with the zombies' decay. "What we ended up doing was a progression," explains Nicotero. "We showed these photos to Frank and said, 'Okay, how far along do you really see that these characters and these creatures go? Will we ever get that far? Will we ever go all the way to the point where there's bone and skull?'" Darabont

EPISODE 2: "GUTS"

Written by Frank Darabont
Directed by Michelle MacLaren

RICK: We survive this by pulling together, not apart.

SYNOPSIS: Lori goes off on her own into the woods to collect mushrooms for dinner. A twig snaps. Birds take flight. And she knows she's not alone. A hand covers her mouth so she can't scream, but it's no Walker. It's Shane taking the moment for a secret rendezvous. Their passionate kisses are interrupted when he opens her shirt to

reveal Rick's wedding ring that she still wears around her neck. After she takes it off, the two make love in the forest, unaware that her husband is alive and trapped in a tank in Atlanta.

The voice coming in over the tank's CB offers to help Rick out of his situation, directing him to a safe escape route while the Walkers are distracted by the horse they're making into a meal. Rick takes a weapon and a grenade from the dead soldier beside him and makes a run for freedom, leaving his weapons bag behind on the street. He fires a round of shots at the Walkers before meeting up with his savior, Glenn.

Glenn brings Rick to the department store where the rest of his group waits.

CONTINUED

Andrea, Jacqui, T-Dog, and Morales had come into the city with Glenn to scavenge supplies, hoping to slip out without incident. They are all now trapped because Rick's gunfire has attracted more Geeks (as Glenn calls them) to the area.

More gunfire draws everyone to the roof, where they find another member of the group, Merle Dixon, firing on the Geeks below. The neo-Nazi bigot spews racist, hate-fueled language, lashing out at T-Dog and threatening him with a gun in an attempt to take charge of the group. Rick decks Merle, handcuffing him to a pipe so they

can deal with the larger issue of being trapped in a building surrounded by the living dead.

When the sewers beneath the building fail to provide an escape route, Rick comes up with a new plan. The trapped survivors pull the bodies of two Geeks they killed into the building. Rick takes a moment to mourn their deaths before horrifically tearing into their bodies with an ax. He and Glenn cover themselves in the remains of the dead to hide their scent so they can slip past the undead to get to a truck at a nearby construction site. The plan works until a downburst washes the smell off Rick and Glenn, who have to run to make it to the vehicle.

In the rush to leave, T-Dog drops the key to the handcuffs holding Merle. He scrambles frantically to grab it but the key falls out of reach. With the undead about to enter the building, T-Dog is forced to leave behind the man that had nothing but hate

for him, but he still manages to chain the door shut to keep the undead from getting to Merle.

Glenn steals a car, setting off its alarm to draw the undead away with noise as Rick pulls the truck up to the store. Andrea, Jacqui, T-Dog, and Morales load up, and they head out of the city to safety, while Merle struggles to break free on the roof.

responded by explaining that the pilot was set about six weeks after the outbreak, which allowed the team to gauge where to start. It also gave them room to grow.

Another element to consider was not just the time from the initial outbreak, but the time of day the series would be filming. Traditional zombie movies are set at night to enhance the mood and build tension with darkness and shadow. "It's what you don't see versus what you see," Nicotero says. But in keeping with its atypical focus, *The Walking Dead* would do things differently. "We're going to be shooting in Atlanta, in broad daylight, in the sun. So, the makeups had to hold up, and they had to look good."

The makeup design team went to work creating zombie faces using a combination of contact lenses, dentures, and prosthetics. For the most part, they would stick to a bit of exposed skin, but not a lot of blood, because the design

ABOVE: Three-dimensional transfers are placed on the skin of zombie extras to simulate decay in a time-saving makeup application process.

wasn't about the gore factor. The plan was for a slow peeling away of the skin to match the natural state of decay. Nicotero then sat down with the KNB EFX in-house designer John Wheaton and developed a progression of looks in the range he and Darabont had discussed.

Every step along the way, Nicotero drew inspiration from the work of Romero. But he had many options his mentor never would have imagined in the late 1960s. "The materials have certainly advanced over the last twenty-five years," Nicotero admits, noting that silicone prosthetics and 3-D transfers make his job considerably easier. "3-D transfers are like a [temporary] tattoo, where you wet it, peel the backing off, and *Ta-da!* you have a tattoo."

The KNB EFX team manufactures three-dimensional tattoos that can go on quickly and be color-matched to an actor's skin tone. Makeup artists do not have to paint an actor's whole face, but instead can put on a patchwork of wounds, creating different zombie looks depending on the way they use the material. "We could mix and match them so on our day, we would have thirty or forty people come in," says Nicotero. "One would walk into the trailer, and I'd sort of look at him and go, 'Yeah, okay, I know what I want to do with you.' Then we'd go and prep the pieces, and we'd do the makeup."

Every day, the crew had new background actors and new characters, so they didn't have to worry about the continuity of each zombie's look. The flexibility of the makeup was particularly important for a series of this magnitude; as Nicotero says, "You have scenes where there are a hundred and fifty zombies—you break it down to twenty featured, forty mid-ground, and ninety background. What we wanted to do was see how quickly we could put together makeups that looked great."

They began by testing on people who worked in the shop, trying different approaches to the makeup and different looks to achieve before moving on to the actors. Lighting was very important in the tests, as it provided valuable information for their design. "It accentuated the cheekbones and then all of a sudden, the eyes look really deeply set in," Nicotero explains. "So this gave us a good indication of the kind of people that we wanted to use in the prosthetics. We want people with big eyes. We want people with good cheekbones. And maybe not necessarily large noses so that we could accentuate the cheekbones and the brow, and de-emphasize the nose. The big eyes were good, because then the contact lenses really stood out."

Every portion of the face was examined in contemplation of the overall look of the makeup and the storytelling aspect as well. Nicotero already had a wealth of information at his disposal from prior experience working on zombie projects, and he used all of that in the creation of this latest look, as well as referencing the source material. "The zombies' primary weapon is their teeth," he notes. "If you look at the artwork in the graphic novel, the teeth are always exposed . . . [in] this kind of menacing, skull-like sneer."

Although it should be no surprise that the makeup artists would look to the original material for inspiration, it was an honor that caught Charlie Adlard off guard. "One of the best compliments they were paying me when I

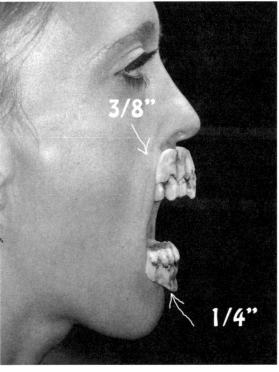

ABOVE: A page from issue no. 8 shows the emphasis on the teeth the makeup team aspired to re-create for the series. Dentures were refitted when necessary to lay flush against the chin.

"I'M A POLICEMAN. I'LL HELP YOU. DON'T BE AFRAID, OKAY? . . . LITTLE GIRL?"

Little Girl
Zombie
Stage 1
Design 1a

KNB EFX
GROUP INC.

WHEATCH
2010

Little Girl
Zombie
Stage 1
Design 1b

KNB EFX
GROUP INC.

WHEATCH
2010

She turns. Staring at him with deep, sunken eyes. Flesh drawn tight on skull and bone. Lips torn away, leaving just a snarl of teeth. She's got braces. Clots of old decayed meat caught in the metal. She's dead. Not sick. Not dressed up for Halloween. Dead.

The opening minutes of the pilot episode feature a zombie kill shot that sets the tone for the series and immediately informs the viewers of exactly the type of TV show they are about to experience. Alone in a derelict gas station, Rick Grimes comes across a little girl whom he believes to be an innocent, abandoned victim. And while it is true that she is a victim, her innocence is gone. The girl is one of the undead, and when she moves on Rick, he is forced to shoot her in the head to stop her from attacking. It is not something seen on TV every day, and it almost didn't appear on-screen.

"In the original draft of the script, you are never supposed to see the little girl zombie that quickly," says Greg Nicotero. "If I remember correctly, what happened was it was kind of a teaser where Rick's in the gas station and we start to see it, but then all of a sudden we cut away. And then we cut back. In the editing room or even as Frank was shooting it, he sort of decided it's much more powerful if we stay with this scene and don't go to the flashback."

Setting up this important scene with such a young actor was challenging, considering the contact lenses and dentures and prosthetic pieces she would have to wear. Nicotero only has so much tolerance for an adult actor who complains about a job he or she signed up for, but he has all the patience in the world when it comes to a child. "What was most important to me," he says, "was to make sure that she was as comfortable as she could be the day we shot." He suggested to the producers that they have the young actress come to the set a couple days early to try on the teeth and the contact lenses so she could get familiar with them.

"The contact lenses and dentures are not the most comfortable things in the world," Nicotero admits. "Especially with her dentures, because the idea was the dentures were supposed to push the corner of her mouth, as if somebody took a big giant bite out of the side of her cheek and revealed the teeth." The dentures also had fake braces. Nicotero wanted her to get used to everything so that when it came time for her to act, her mind would be clear.

Nicotero feels that the extra time she had to try out the makeup made a big difference on the day of filming: "It was a hundred degrees out. It was sticky. She was drooling all of the time because the way we made the dentures, it actually distorted the lip and made the lip look torn and ragged. . . . At one point she just sat there, and there was bloody drool coming out the corner of her mouth. I kept saying, 'Are you okay?' 'Yes, I'm fine.' So we kept her as comfortable as we could, and she did an amazing job."

In this case, it was even more important to do whatever they could through visual effects so that the young actress did not experience any more discomfort than was absolutely necessary. "You're not going to put a squib on the back of a seven-year-old girl's head," says Sam Nicholson. "In that case, there's just no other option. So if you're going to resort to visual effects, it has got to look perfectly real. And it's got to

CONTINUED

blend perfectly with all of the practical effects that Greg's doing on set. When you get different artistic departments like prosthetics and visual effects and mechanical effects to all work perfectly in unison where you can rely on anyone that you want for the best possible result, it's great."

ABOVE: Blood splatter was added digitally rather than using the makeup team's blood-spray rig to avoid making the young actress more uncomfortable.

PREVIOUS SPREAD: Design concepts for the little girl zombie played by Addy Miller.

was on set," he recalls, "was … that they were basing the look of the zombies from the comic book. They didn't have to do that. But they thought the way that Tony and I drew zombies was strong enough that they could actually be influenced by it and, hopefully, make it show in the series."

The graphic novel was not Nicotero's sole inspiration for focusing on the teeth: The decision was also based on real-world research. Having worked extensively with re-creating bodies in various forms over his career, he has picked up a certain amount of anatomical knowledge necessary for the job. "If you look at old photos of mummified remains and corpses that have been preserved, the lips have always kind of stretched," he says. "It's like the skin gets really tight and everything's pulled back. They played that up in the graphic novel, and it was something that I had always thought would be really interesting; to be able to reveal the teeth as something potentially frightening."

To achieve that look for the series, KNB constructed prosthetic dentures that would fit over the actors' lips. This created an optical illusion that the skin was pulling back from the mouth, when in reality the mouth was growing beyond the face.

In addition to the individual 3-D "tattoos," they also created full-scale masks for the background zombies to wear, for practical reasons. Not every zombie would require a custom look, and the crew had to cut corners whenever possible for zombies that weren't going to be prominently featured. "We just didn't have the resources to do a hundred and fifty makeups

in one day," Nicotero explains. "We had five makeup people, and then some additionals as we shot. What we ended up doing was sculpting a variety of masks, and we kept them kind of generic looking so that then we could paint them and make them look a little bit different."

Those basic masks provided multiple grotesque faces to fill a given scene. The masks were sculpted over approximations of skulls so the team could trim foam or silicone away to reveal more bone and make them a little creepier. "It certainly was challenging," Nicotero recalls, "because we had all this stuff to make in a very short time. And we had only read the pilot episode. We hadn't gotten the other scripts while we were prepping, because it was February and we weren't shooting till June. We had to anticipate what we were going to do."

The zombie look they achieved not only came through on the screen, but was obvious in person as well, which sometimes led to humorous results. As Executive Producer David Alpert recalls: "One of the most surreal moments I ever had was in downtown Atlanta shooting the pilot. We had this whole scene where there are basically two hundred zombies that come around the corner to attack the horse. I go into the zombie holding area where they're all getting their makeup done, but they're all waiting. So all of the people who are finished are sitting in this large conference room, and you're seeing zombies on cell phones, zombies reading the paper, zombies eating their lunch. It was bizarre."

Once KNB EFX had the bodies set, they turned their attention to something a

ABOVE: Nicotero dresses a sculpted corpse with blood for maximum impact.

little deeper: blood. No matter how much the producers, the critics, and the fans talk up *The Walking Dead*'s living characters, a lot of people tune in for the gore. You can't have a zombie tale without it getting a little messy.

Going from living to undead is a violent process. At minimum, a single bite is necessary to do the deed, but the Walkers rarely stop there. Victims who are not completely devoured will rise again, with their bodies beginning their decay from whatever state they were in when they died. The zombies of *The Walking Dead* needed to visually convey the violence that had ended their lives so that every corpse told a story.

"One of the things I always felt was important about zombie stuff is conveying violence with how the blood is dressed," says Nicotero. "You can't take a brush and brush blood on because it doesn't look organic. So one of the things that we always did was to simulate violence by having blood spray up onto their faces. The idea was that a zombie would come in and bite and blood would spray and spatter everywhere. When you look at the makeup and you see the little spatters of blood and the bite wound, it feels more authentic. It looks like this guy was attacked and was fighting his way off and blood was spraying, splattering him. But he didn't survive."

Beyond the blood left behind on the exterior, the reanimated corpses still have plasma in their veins, which makes the gore-filled kill shots more spectacular. These deaths might go by in a blink on-screen, but they take careful planning and a lot of work to pull off. Over the years, Nicotero has learned the cardinal rule about this effect: "Blood gags are inherently unpredictable." But the inability to rely on the blood to do what the production needs is not the only problem.

In the past, convincing "blood gags" required the use of a squib, a miniature explosive device placed on an actor's body to simulate a gunshot or other impact wound. These have been largely phased out in current productions for practical reasons. In the 1970s when Romero was working on his second masterpiece in the *Dead* series, *Dawn of the Dead*, there were no

ABOVE: The compressed air blood-spray rig allowed the crew to film the gags on location with minimal visual effects added later.

rules governing the use of squibs. They could be placed on anyone, including regular extras with no experience with the devices. Today it has to be a stunt person, which is cost-prohibitive on a project with dozens of zombie extras being gunned down and hacked to death. And even with stunt people, the method isn't perfect. "On a TV schedule, we had eight days per episode," Nicotero explains. "There are certain realities that you have to deal with. Reality number one is to do a squib on somebody's head and spray blood all over everything and then go in and clean it all up and spend twenty minutes to reset it—which is fast—isn't practical."

Nicotero determined that the spray resulting from a zombie head wound needed to fit two parameters: "It has to be instantaneous, and it has to spray outward so that we see it." With squibs, often the device would have to be placed on the back of the actor's head for safety reasons, which meant that the blood would shoot backward and thus out of the main visual field.

With those factors in mind, the effects team built a vest with a reservoir in the back holding a volume of blood that could instantaneously spray outward. But the minor blast that would result from detonating a charge in the blood reservoir would atomize the liquid, so the team needed some instrument that would force all of the liquid out as visible spatter. They ended up using a bellowslike device to force air into the vest and displace the liquid. As Nicotero explains, "We had a ten-foot tube, and you would stomp on the bellows and that would allow all the air in the tube to force the liquid out instantly. It's not an explosive squib, it's just

ZOMBIE SCHOOL

ABOVE: Graduates of the Class of 2010 Zombie School as they shuffle out into the world.

"Once when my dad and I returned to the A/C tent, a zombie actor was laying on the ground to cool off, but we thought she was one of Greg's mannequins, until she sat up! So when little Noah [Lomax] came into the tent, we said, 'Hey, Noah, give that mannequin a kick, it is squishy!' So he went over to look and the actor—who was back laying perfectly still by then—jumped up and scared him to death! We laughed so hard!"

—**Chandler Riggs**

To create the perfect zombie, it's not just what's on the outside that counts. The actors underneath the makeup have to be up to the challenge of physically embodying the creature they are playing. Frank Darabont has always appreciated the unsung talents of background extras, but they are absolutely essential to making *The Walking Dead* work.

"Aside from your basic street scene, where people are walking around in the background or in the back of a restaurant, extras are far more crucial to a movie than people sometimes assume," Darabont notes. "For example, in *The Green Mile*, when Michael Jeter is electrocuted and it all goes wrong, I needed a room full of people to really be actors. To really be reacting. To really be part of the scene and not just furniture in the background."

It's the same on most of Darabont's projects. In *The Mist*, a store full of people are on-screen throughout the entire movie. That required more than just the simple directions of telling them where to stand and when to move. "You gather them together, and you elicit their best work as well," Darabont says. "You explain to them what you're going to be expecting on the day when they're on set. When you do that, people get it, and they do realize this is going to be different than other extra work they've done. That can be tremendously fun, because then they become part of the unit as well."

Darabont wanted to do something similar with *The Walking Dead*, especially because of a warning about working with zombie extras that Nicotero had previously shared with him. Darabont explains, "He said George Romero once said to him the problem with having extras show up cold on the set is they don't really have any grounding in how to behave as a zombie. Then the danger is you show them what you want, and then you have a hundred people all doing exactly the same thing."

This led to the creation of a "zombie school" where the background extras received special training for their task. At first, the idea didn't go over so well with all parties. "I had originally thought that the idea of a zombie school seemed like a lot of work," Greg Nicotero admits. He recalls that the line producer, Tom Luse, was one of the major proponents for the classes and helped convince him. It wasn't that Nicotero thought the idea was bad; it was just that there was already so much to do, and a three-day commitment for training extras seemed overwhelming.

Eventually, Nicotero acquiesced and flew in to Atlanta early to work with the extras. "In retrospect," he admits, "it made such a difference. I'm so glad that we did it, because it allowed me to get a preview of who the good performers were, who the great faces were, and who the not-too-good performers were."

Nicotero cut together a short demo reel of what he considered to be great zombie scenes in other projects. He sent the tape to Darabont to make sure they were on the same page, and the producer added his own suggestions so they could finalize the presentation piece to use for inspiration. Armed with that tape, Nicotero and a dance movement choreographer worked with twenty extras at a time.

CONTINUED

The first objective was to have the extras simply move from one side of the room to the other in their own interpretations of a zombie. Nicotero picked out the ones who had the best looks and gave suggestions to enhance the character. "Instead of demonstrating it, we always tried to get them in tune with what looked good," he says. "We came up with a bunch of ideas, like we would set up a row of chairs and say, 'Okay, sit in the chair. You're dead. Now wake up and move around.' We put chairs in the middle of the room, and we'd see how they just navigated. As we did it, we got better and better at finding the people who were great and the people who looked good. There were a couple of people I just loved."

This was particularly important since Nicotero already knew one very important lesson about filming zombie extras: "Nothing will kill a zombie crowd scene faster than two or three people really performing badly." The eye naturally drifts to anything that looks out of place, so the fear became that, in a highly choreographed street scene, any individual who was too exaggerated or too forced would steal all focus from the action.

"One of the things I said to the people at zombie school was, 'If I give your zombie a nickname, then you're fucked,'" Nicotero notes. A nickname meant the actor was doing something too recognizable. In the case of a zombie stomping around too heavily, he would call that person the "Get the Hell Out of My Yard" zombie. If one of the extras was dragging his feet, he became the "Ice-skating" zombie.

Nicotero graded the performances and worked with the casting people to find the right look. Eventually, he wound up handpicking the zombie extras for every scene, so he knew exactly what kind of performance to expect.

"It was a really smart way to go," Darabont notes, "because we had sort of a core group of extras, and you could put them out there in front of the camera and not get the same thing. They all feel like they have individual personalities." Darabont is not only speaking for the pilot episode he directed. He says that he has witnessed these moments in every episode of the series. Each of the different directors was able to create these moments, but Darabont is sure to give credit where credit is due. "It's all because of zombie school, really," he admits. "And Greg's knack for knowing what looks right and what doesn't. And, of course, he has my proxy because we both come from the same place. Our brains spring from the same geek background."

ABOVE: One of the many different kill shots designed by the production team.

air. So you're not endangering anyone, and the reset is you just fill the reservoir again."

This method was used extensively in the pilot and the campsite zombie attack in episode 4. Not only did it allow for an easier setup, but the device had the added bonus of giving the blood directionality. To enhance the effect, the team added Styrofoam peanuts to the blood to give it a chunkier look. Since the material wouldn't absorb the liquid, it stayed light enough to explode outward in a dramatic fashion.

Still, some scenes required even more flexibility with the blood spatter. In many cases, the visual effects department came in to enhance or create the look of the kill shot. The sequence at the opening of episode 2, for example, required

Rick to run through the street shooting almost a dozen Walkers in the head to achieve safe passage. To create this type of scene with practical effects would be a challenge in camera blocking. For the cameraperson to capture the blood spray at the right moment before moving on to the next victim and the next as actor Andrew Lincoln runs through the street would have required detailed choreography. But adding the blood later allowed for more freedom of movement.

Even with Nicotero's practical solution for spraying blood, the visual effects team at Stargate Studios still had work to do to come in and enhance the look. Stargate CEO and Visual Effects Supervisor Sam Nicholson agreed with

Nicotero that they should rely on live blood effects whenever possible, but everyone understood that it would not always be a perfect option. "Sometimes it would be too liquid or too red or too whatever," says Nicholson, "and we can go back in and perfect it. So the black zombie blood was a very fine-tuned thing in every single show. It's the same blood. If it just happens to catch the light backlit or whatever, and it's too red, we just take the red down. And, if it splats the wrong way or if it detracts from the performance because it's too big, then we reduce it. If it's too small, then we make it bigger." Stargate has an impressive library of blood hits and liquid dynamics in 3-D; they can perfect and watch every drop to determine where it needs to go in the final scene.

The visual effects blood work requires considerable thought. Like every other element of production, the blood tells a story, but it also needs to allow the dramatic show's story line to come through on its own. As a result, the visual effects team has to be precise about how much of an effect to add and when to back off.

"If it's so over the top, it steals from the performance," says Nicholson. "If the visual effect overrides the performance, then we haven't done our job right . . . We should be invisible. The visual effects are really the frame *around* the picture—they're not the picture. That's a common flaw with visual effects. It's like a cake with too much icing on it. It's got to be just the right amount, and then it works."

Just because the work is precisely calibrated doesn't mean it can't be fun. Visual Effects Supervisor Jason Sperling was a fan of the comic book series before the studio started working on the production. He, in particular, looks forward to the variety of effects they will be creating to bring the comic to life. "Something that actually excites me with *The Walking Dead* is all of the head shots and the kill shots," he says. "I know that, ultimately, what zombie fans enjoy is a good zombie killing. I think [. . .] we brought new ideas to almost every instance of a kill shot."

Sperling's excitement over kills has nothing to do with some deep-rooted bloodlust. He enjoys the opportunity to take what can be staged on set and make it bigger. One of his personal highlights from the first season is a brief blink-and-you-miss-it moment. Sperling explains: "When they're running out of the CDC and Daryl takes this axe and swings at a zombie—initially it was just supposed to be kind of a 'hit the zombie on the head and the zombie falls over.' But we were able to slice that head completely off and roll it onto the ground, and it makes for a really awesome zombie killing moment. I think our artists really took the challenge of trying to make each head shot unique enough that I don't think I ever got tired of seeing zombie deaths."

"As far as we're concerned, we've only covered a portion of the alphabet, and we have *A* to *Z* to go through yet," adds Nicholson. "There are many different ways to kill a zombie."

OPPOSITE: As the series continues, the writers, directors, and makeup and visual effects teams will need to continue to push the envelope in designing exciting and gruesome zombie kill shots.

FOUR

POPULATING THE WORLD OF *THE WALKING DEAD*

The zombies may be the reason people first check out *The Walking Dead*, but it's the characters that convince them to stay. Readers and viewers get to be witnesses to a world stripped of the trappings of our consumer culture, where life-and-death decisions are made every single day and the survivors of this mysterious epidemic are trapped in a crucible of emotional turmoil. "The focus is really on this group of characters," notes Frank Darabont. "It's tough, edgy, adult material, and it really draws me in very much on that level. The zombies are the frosting on the cake, but the main meal is these characters that I believe we get tremendously invested in."

The Walking Dead is an ensemble piece centered on the unifying character of Rick Grimes. We see the new postapocalyptic world largely through his eyes as the events change this small-town sheriff's deputy dramatically over the course of the comic book series. He goes from firmly believing that anyone who commits murder should be punished by death, to committing murder himself to ensure the safety of his family and his people.

Adapting this story and this character for the small screen required the production team, and especially Robert Kirkman, to step back and examine Rick at the start of this new journey. "Rick in the TV show is very much like the Rick in the first twelve issues or so [of the comic]," Kirkman says. "He's still trying to find his way and still trying to figure out how this world works. He's still essentially good. The Rick in the comic now has allowed this world to taint him. He makes rash decisions. He'll do anything to protect his people and his son. Oftentimes he makes bad decisions in order to do that. He's a very different character."

These two disparate versions of Rick Grimes presented a challenge for Kirkman when he wrote the fourth episode of season 1, "Vatos." In that story, Rick, T-Dog, and Daryl capture one of the members of the gang holding Glenn hostage. Daryl is more than willing to do whatever it takes to get information out of the guy—including torture, a decision that Rick must wrestle with in the episode. "There were a lot of times where I would go, 'Yeah. Rick would totally do this,'" says Kirkman. "But I'd have to stop myself and say, 'No. Rick wouldn't

just kill that guy. The TV Rick hasn't gotten to that point yet. You're writing Comic Book Rick. Calm down. He's the kinder, gentler Rick.' I do have to constantly remind myself of that when I'm working on the TV show."

ABOVE: In his cowboy-style deputy's hat and uniform, Rick Grimes has come to represent the prototypical American lawman in a situation that far exceeds his small-town training.

PREVIOUS SPREAD: Though *The Walking Dead* boasts a talented ensemble cast, much of the series rests on the shoulders of sheriff's deputy, Rick Grimes as portrayed by Andrew Lincoln.

The qualities that define Rick as a heroic lead at the opening of the series will make his potential downfall all the more dramatic. It's not a coincidence that he is a sheriff's deputy. The uniform he wears is a constant reminder that he is the law. In both the comic and the TV show, he assumes the mantle of leadership from Shane rather quickly. He might only be a deputy from a small town, but he is the one everyone looks to. It is no small moment in the comic book when he passes his deputy's hat on to his son. It is just as meaningful when the group later

RICK SHERIFF UNIFORM   SC 1;2;3
↓

* ⑧ BULLET PROOF VEST
Description opp. page.

⑨ UNIFORM JKT: HORACE SMALL   47 — 105
* SHERIFF DEPT.   NG
Drk brn w/side zips & sheriffs   M/M   dept
badge
on sleeves

① UNDER SHIRT : CALVIN KLEIN

Teched WHITE : sh/sl ; crew neck

② UNIFORM SHIRT: LAW PRO   MED ⑮ — ⑮½

BEIGE W/DRK BRN EPAULETTES: sh/sl @ABF
→ SHERIFF'S DEPT BADGES SEWN ON SLEEVES (upper)

③ UNIFORM PANTS : FLYING CROSS   ㉜REG

DRK BROWN W/BEIGE 'TUX'/SIDE STRIPE
(vertical)

④ BELT : 0100701/010   ㉞/35
BLACK leather   (right hand threading)

⑤ SHOES : Justin STYLE 2222   10½

BROWN / 'COWBOY' BOOTS   ⑦ SOCKS :
TALL WHITE — BOOT

⑥ HAT : STETSON   7¼
4' BRIM 22 CHOCOLATE

DRK BRN w/gold DOUBLE ROPE & ACORNS (shiny)
HOLE PRE-MADE TO ATTACH 'sheriff star badge'

exchanges their regular clothes for prison uniforms, as the comic story line evolves.

It's the myriad of qualities Rick possesses that first attracted Darabont to this particular zombie project. "I love Rick Grimes," Darabont proclaims. "He's my favorite kind of lead character. He's the kind of guy who was trying to do the right thing even when circumstances are against him and even when doing the right thing doesn't always turn out the right way. The right thing can sometimes blow up in your face. It can

ABOVE: Andrew Lincoln plays a version of Rick Grimes very close to the one in the early issues of the comic.

backfire on you. But the intention of a person like that who is trying to keep it together—trying to keep his grace and his good intentions in impossible circumstances—that appeals to me greatly."

From the perspective of the storyteller, Darabont enjoys making the cracks form on a character. "There has to be some complexity and depth," he says. "You really have to see the dark side of somebody, as well, to understand them and, indeed, to love them. So Rick winds up being a very complex character. Certainly, the long-range narrative that Robert Kirkman

has proposed definitely deconstructs this poor man in some pretty substantial ways."

Casting directors Sharon Bialy and Sherry Thomas were challenged to find an actor who could embody such a noble character at the onset before the writers put him through the wringer. As Bialy explains, "You needed someone to portray a hero who was a good and honest man, who didn't have the traditional flaws of a hero. He had high moral values. And I think the producers did not want someone who was recognizable from another show so that you really created this character and had him come alive from the graphic novel. You also needed the level of actor who could carry the show and be the lead of the show. That's a hard combo to find."

The edict to find an actor unfamiliar to American TV audiences came from the network itself. "They are actor-driven, not star-driven," Bialy says of AMC. "The aesthetic made our job easier, because they care about the best actor, and some of the people that they respond positively to, other networks wouldn't."

Although Bialy and Thomas read many local actors for what has become a quintessentially American role, they had to cross the pond fairly late in the casting process to find their perfect Rick Grimes. While Andrew Lincoln certainly wasn't unknown to movie audiences (who would recognize him from *Love Actually*), the casting directors felt that American television viewers might not be as familiar with him. They contacted his agent in London, and Lincoln self-taped his audition in his apartment and sent it to Bialy and Thomas. The casting agents felt he was perfect for the part. The only

POPULATING THE WORLD OF *THE WALKING DEAD*   97

problem was that, as the father of a young child, he wasn't sure he could pursue the role.

"We were quite aggressive that he needed to do it," Thomas admits. They convinced him to come out to Los Angeles for a screen test with Jon Bernthal (Shane), which they wound up shooting in Darabont's garage. "I think I was holding the camera light and Sherry was holding the mic," Bialy says. "There was a sound operator there, but there wasn't enough money to do a full screen test like we had the first round, so we did it all in Frank's garage."

Darabont sat the two actors in a Passat posing as a police car, and shot a scene of them talking. "Andy just was immediately the guy," he says. "He had the depth. He had the ineffable quality of 'you want to know what this guy is thinking.' I think with truly great screen presences, there's a little bit of mystery to them. You want to know what's going on in their head. He draws you in instead of telling you everything."

Bialy also gets the appeal. "Part of it is also matching up the rhythm of the language, the way Frank writes," she says. "Somehow Andy got that instinctually."

It helped that the actors trusted one another immediately, and that trust came through on-screen. Bernthal, who had already been cast as Shane, had gone through the process with different scene partners, and the casting directors cite his warmth and inviting attitude toward Lincoln as beneficial to the process. "I think also the pressure was off with Jon," Thomas adds. "He had the job. So he was very able to just really be in the moment and let Andrew shine and do his thing."

ABOVE: Jon Bernthal portrays the intense Shane Walsh, who has already outlived his comic counterpart by episode 5.

AMC agreed, and Lincoln was cast into the role, quickly making it his own. "He really inhabited that role," says Executive Producer David Alpert. "He's such a great actor. He really just settled into that role and adopted it, taking on the tone. Even his posture changes when he's in character. It's kind of an amazing thing."

The lead was one of the last roles the casting directors filled. Once they had their Rick Grimes, the final piece of the puzzle fell into place. It was the end of a long, nontraditional process buoyed along by Darabont's enthusiasm. As Bialy explains, "Frank loves actors, so he doesn't always want to be in the room with them the first time, because he just falls in love with everybody. He needs a little distance. He really likes to watch the audition on a big screen so he can really focus and pay attention."

In Hollywood, actors tend to start the audition process with the producers and director in the room. Certainly bigger name celebrities don't come in just for the casting directors. But

ABOVE: Lori, as played by Sarah Wayne Callies, is torn between two men while struggling to raise her child in a postapocalyptic world.

Darabont's preference to see everyone on-screen first helped narrow the field to actors who were interested enough in the part to do something they wouldn't normally consider.

"In this situation," Bialy explains, "many of the actors had to come in for the casting director, which they may not have done in a long time. All of the actors who were cast swallowed their egos and went through the process because they really loved it. I think that's maybe one of the reasons it all worked out, because the whole process was done with such care. We spent a very long time with each actor. Oftentimes, in the television world, you're in and out really quickly, but Sherry or I would spend a half-hour or forty-five minutes with each actor."

Certainly, in television, actors like Sarah Wayne Callies, who had played the female lead in the popular series *Prison Break*, were not accustomed to coming in to see casting directors. But the series is better for it. Alpert notes, "You could not ask for a nicer person, or a more talented actress. She has a real intelligence and

empathy that comes through in real life, but also helps with the [on-screen] situation."

Alpert believes those traits are important in the actress who plays Lori Grimes, because her character is such a challenge as an empathic figure. He explains, "She's obviously done something—in the worst-case scenario, it's as understandable as it could be—but it's one of the biggest betrayals you can do. The crazy thing is, you still like her. And that's hard. We see her sleep with Shane, and we still like her, because she allows us to understand. She really does."

Lori Grimes is the apex of the Rick–Lori–Shane triangle. But more than that, she and her son serve as the motivation for almost every action both of these men take. At the same time, she has to be a strong character on her own, or she will fall into a simple damsel-in-distress role. It's very important that she can defend herself against zombies, and even against Shane. She holds her own, standing up for her beliefs over the course of the first six episodes, but giving in when she knows her point has been made.

All the characters in Kirkman's comic go through tragic and traumatic experiences that affect them deeply. But somewhere along the way, the comic book story shifts focus from Rick Grimes onto his son. Carl's journey is heartbreaking. No matter what Rick does to protect him, there is no question that the terrifying world in which he now has to grow up is having its effect on him. From shooting Shane to protect his father, to carrying out other violent precautionary acts because he's the only one who can, Carl wears his dad's deputy hat with

RICK-LORI-SHANE

ABOVE: The relationship at the core of the postapocalyptic story is a love triangle, with Lori at its core.

The Walking Dead TV series takes some detours from the established story, but it also builds off the world created in the comic book. By expanding on certain story lines and characters, it allows the writing team to create entirely new paths to explore. Nowhere is that more noticeable than in the love triangle that has Lori Grimes caught between her husband, Rick, and his best friend, Shane.

The triangle is established in the comic series, but ends abruptly at the close of issue 6 with Shane's death. In the small-screen version, Shane has already outlived his comic counterpart when the survivors move on from their camp in episode 5. This gives the writers a wealth of new stories to tell in the second season. "The show, to a certain extent, is correcting some things that I may have done differently in hindsight," says Robert Kirkman. "Because I didn't know how long the comic book would last, I tried to tell as much story as I could as quickly as I could in those early issues.

"While the Shane–Rick–Lori love triangle seems like it would be a rich thing that you could mine stories out of for years," he continues, "I got through it in six issues and moved on. There's very little Shane in the comic book. But that was done

CONTINUED

because I didn't know if there would be a seventh issue. I didn't know if there would be a tenth issue. In hindsight, knowing that I would have been able to do the book for a good long time, I might have stretched that stuff out. With the show we're actually able to do that."

Rick: Last thing she said this morning? "Sometimes I wonder if you even care about us at all." She said that in front of our kid. Imagine going to school with that in your head. The difference between men and women. I would never say something that cruel to her, and certainly not in front of Carl.

ABOVE: Much of the tension in the series comes from Rick and Shane jockeying for a leadership position in the camp, just as they do in the early comic issues.

We see the new potential for storytelling the first time Rick and Shane are on-screen together. The comic book opens mid-gunfight that sends Rick directly into his coma. Any backstory comes after Shane and Lori's relationship begins on the road to Atlanta, and even then only in flashbacks after his death. By opening the TV series with Rick confiding in his friend about his marriage problems, Darabont and the writing team establish that any threat to the marriage is not solely a reaction to the zombie apocalypse. It could simply be a typical argument any couple might have, but it leaves the audience wondering what would have happened in the Grimes's marriage had the world not ended.

Rick and Lori are very much alike in their motivation to protect others. The first conversation the audience sees between Lori and Shane is her insisting that they should put signs up on the interstate to warn people away from the city. But more importantly, her insistence about going off on her own to put up the signs mirrors Rick's desire to go back into Atlanta, not just to get the guns and rescue Merle, but to get the walkie-talkie that will allow him to warn Morgan away. In the first case, Shane is able to talk Lori out of her plan by reminding her she needs to stay at camp for Carl's sake. Neither she nor Shane has the same luck when it comes to convincing Rick not to go back into the city.

CONTINUED

Lori: Shut up. Just don't. My husband's back. He's alive.

Shane: He's my best friend. You think I'm not happy about that?

Lori: Why would you be? You're the one who told me he died.

The decision for Rick to return to Atlanta has far-reaching consequences for the camp, and it gives Lori time to establish her new boundaries with Shane without her husband around. It also comments greatly on all three characters. "That's a very difficult choice to make," says Gale Anne Hurd. "And certainly it shows the sort of triangle among Shane, Rick, and Lori. That's not a decision Shane would make. Shane liked to make the value judgment that 'Rick's not really as good a father or a husband as I would be. I would never compromise their safety or the safety of the group that we have here to do something that may not be a success. That more than likely, the odds are against the mission's success.'"

Later, the moment in the woods when Shane has Rick in his gun sights mimics a page straight from the comic book. But in the comic, the confrontation is much more direct, with Rick knowing he's in trouble. It also leads to Shane's death. Instead, on the show, Dale is a witness to what Shane plays off as a near accident, but it ends with

ABOVE: Lori is often torn between siding with her husband and agreeing with Shane. Her decisions are often based on her marital relationship rather than her true beliefs.

him very much alive. The decision to keep Shane around will greatly affect the future of the series. "There's much more drama to be mined," Hurd says. "We find out not only more about Shane, we find out more about Lori and Rick, their relationship, as well as what kind of a father Rick is to Carl. There are times you wonder—Shane actually

seems like he's more comfortable being a father to Carl than Rick is. Shane's able to let his hair down and go try to catch frogs with Carl. You just can't imagine Rick doing that. And yet, at the same time, you can't imagine Rick being as brutal, beating someone up as Shane does when

ABOVE: Carl's relationship with the men vying for his mother's heart is often a source of tension between all three adults.

he almost kills Ed [after he sees the man strike his wife, Carol]. There are two sides of Shane. He can be the most fun person to be around, but he also has a very dark, violent streak. Would he have pulled the trigger and shot Rick when they were out in the woods if Dale hadn't been there?"

That darkness comes out later when he tries to force himself on Lori in the CDC. It's another moment that parallels the comic, when Lori leaves scratch marks on his face. In the comic, her reaction is in response to Shane punching her husband in front of everyone. In the TV series, she does it to protect herself, but still keeps the secret of what he tried to do to her.

"The Rick, Lori, and Shane dynamic is only getting started," Frank Darabont says. "The complications in what is fundamentally kind of a triangle circumstance are really only just getting under way. That's going to be tremendously fun and rewarding to explore in the second season. . . . That's what I mean when I say it's such a character-driven show and that's what turns me on. I'm really excited about exploring that triangle that has developed between these three people. That, to me, is the second season."

pride, accepting the role of protector when he has to, often with horrific consequences.

If the TV show were to stay true to the emotional depth of the comic book character, the casting directors needed a performer ready for the challenge. Chandler Riggs had appeared in a TV

ABOVE: Chandler Riggs on his callback audition: "We did a scene from the comics and I felt like it went well. It was hard to imagine that I would get to be in a cool zombie show!"

movie produced by Gale Anne Hurd called *The Wronged Man*, in which he played Julia Ormond's son. Although the roles are very different, Hurd recognized that the boy had the chops. "He's an actor," she says. "He's not a 'child actor.' He's a real actor. What's really impressive is that even when he's not on camera—if there's an emotional scene—he's crying. Even though the camera's not on him and he knows the camera's not on him, he's that into his character and the drama."

With a confidence unusual for his age, Riggs feels as though he aced every stage of the audition. "A lot of people say that I am a lot like Carl," Riggs notes. "I look like him, I act like him, but I sure hope that I don't go crazy like Carl does in the comics. I do look forward

to being a part of the story, though, and I know that we are in good hands with our storytellers."

One character who Darabont and the show writers have much room to explore is Shane Walsh. Though he only appears in the first six issues of the comic—with a couple cameos later on—his presence is felt throughout the first forty-eight issues. The impact he has on Lori and Rick's relationship survives long past his death and brief resurrection, but that was simply not enough when it came time to creating the television show. The decision was made that the initial story would not come to the same conclusion, at least for a while, as Shane would live to carry on the triangle and bring a new dynamic to the storytelling. As such, it gave viewers a deeper insight into the character they only got a glimpse of in the comic.

"I think that TV Shane is a really interesting character," says Kirkman. Although many of the story beats are similar to those of Shane's comic counterpart, Kirkman found a new appreciation for all the character had given up to protect the family of his best friend and for the guilt he carried for falling in love with Rick's wife. "He was always trying to do the right thing, but everything just got worse and worse for him," Kirkman continues. "I think there are a lot of layers to that that are really interesting and are a lot of fun to explore. It's great that the show can do that and that you don't have to strictly follow what was set forth in the comic."

Jon Bernthal embodies the conflicting emotions—and outright aggression, at times—of a character experiencing deeply personal turmoil on top of the inherent drama of life in a postapocalyptic world. "Jon Bernthal is an unbelievable actor," says Alpert. "He really brings this incredible, aggressive, frustrated alpha-male thing to bear."

As one goes through the cast of *The Walking Dead*, it's hard not to notice how similar many of the actors are to their comic book counterparts. In a world where fan bases follow movie and TV show casting notices with almost obsessive attentiveness, it's surprising to hear that any similarities were purely coincidental. "I was very involved in the casting process from the get-go," says Alpert. "And it really was not anybody's intention. We saw tons of combinations for Shane, Rick, Lori. Everybody. It's funny, because Steven [Yeun] looks so much like Glenn that we often just call him Glenn. He just fits the persona so well."

Not only did the casting directors find an actor that was similar in look to the character, they hired a person that was already a fan of the comic book, thanks to a friend that had turned him on to it years earlier. "I sat there and read the first three volumes in the store," Yeun admits. "At first, I didn't know what to make of it. I remember asking why it was black-and-white and then thinking, 'Man this might be crazy boring.' But page after page, it just kept going and raising the stakes. I think I got into Kirkman's book because it's just a well-written book. It takes on the job of just pumping up the stakes higher and higher. It's pretty great." Yeun notes that having a frame of reference for the character neither helped nor hurt him when he accepted the role, but so far Glenn has stayed fairly true to his comic origins.

"Glenn is someone who's not really aware of how valuable he is to the group," says Hurd. "Perhaps because prior to the zombie apocalypse, he was a pizza delivery guy; not exactly high on the food chain either economically or in

ABOVE: *The Walking Dead* ensemble.

ABOVE: Steven Yeun on his callback: "I walked into [Darabont's] office and did the scene right in front of him. No suits, no crowd, no amphitheater. It was just Frank, his camera, and a couple of other actors. It was awesome. Then I remember getting 'the call' in my car on the way to a commercial audition. I pulled over and just freaked out." (Photos: Steven, Laurie Holden, and Jeffrey DeMunn)

terms of perceived value. But at the same time, when we meet him, he is by far the most skilled survivor. He's the one who, on his own, can go into town and get supplies and come back alive. He's someone who naturally does the right thing, and people trust him. He also still has a sense of humor, which very few people have in this postapocalyptic world. He can still see the irony in other people and in the world."

While not all members of the cast are exact doppelgangers—some bear no resemblance to their comic counterparts whatsoever—the similarities allowed AMC to create a graphic that connected drawings of the comic characters to photos of their TV show counterparts. The artwork, revealed at San Diego Comic-Con, was developed to emphasize that, while the series would diverge from the comic at times, it was still, at its core, true to the comic and those characters the fans already loved.

When it came to casting the role of Morgan Jones, the first living person Rick would meet when he was out of the hospital, the casting directors knew there was only one man for the job: Lennie James. "We're huge fans," says Thomas. "*Huge.* We put him in his first series when he came into town. And then we put him in his next one. And then when we saw this, we told Frank that there's one guy for this. He was the first person that we brought in; the first person that we showed to Frank. And Frank was in total agreement."

Bialy is quick to note that James is a perfect example of what they spoke of when describing the unusual nature of casting the show. Under any other circumstances, there would be no reason for James to read for casting directors who had already placed him twice in other work. They would have brought him right in to read for the producers. It said a lot about the established actor that he had no qualms about coming in to be filmed.

"Lennie didn't have an ego about it," Bialy says. "He came in. He read. Frank wasn't in the room. I think that's the thing that was so interesting about this process. Perhaps there were actors that missed out on a wonderful opportunity because of the nature of the politics of television. It took actors that were willing to throw that away and just look at the material and say, 'I'll do what I have to do.'"

But James wasn't the only person interested in the part of Morgan Jones. Many actors were equally willing to look past the traditional system and read for the role. "Both Sherry and I felt that was probably one of the best roles for an African American male that had come out in a very long time," Bialy says. "We were deluged with actors who wanted to play that role, so we had to keep seeing people. But Frank fell in love with Lennie from day one."

The casting directors weren't the only ones with an idea of whom they wanted to bring into the show. It's a well-known fact that Darabont has an unofficial repertory company of actors he has cast in several projects. In this case, he had parts in mind for Jeffrey DeMunn, Laurie Holden, and Melissa McBride.

"There's a reason you work with people again and again," Darabont says. "The talent certainly is a big factor there. But it's also the pleasure of the experience of working with those kinds of colleagues that sometimes demand that

you look for the roles that you can give those people who've brought such value to the working experience and to the final product in the past. I go, 'Okay what's the Jeff DeMunn part? Where is the Laurie Holden role?' In this case it was a no-brainer to find roles for those two because she's the perfect Andrea and he's the perfect Dale."

Darabont was not just randomly filling parts, though. "He's very specific," says Thomas. "He didn't discuss ten of his actors that he uses in all of his films. He really was very specific, and it was those three that fit in this world. He doesn't try to fit them in if it doesn't work." Bialy echoes her partner's assurance that it's as much about the work as it is the relationships. "Jeffrey's a fantastic actor, so it's not like you're casting your brother," she adds. "The people in his company of actors are all so talented."

DeMunn was performing in *Death of a Salesman* in Dallas when he got the phone call from Darabont asking if he wanted to come to Atlanta and kill zombies. "I knew nothing about the graphic novel," DeMunn says. "I knew nothing about the show or the other actors. I didn't know a thing. It would be as if someone who is a really good chef says, 'Do you want to come eat at our place on Friday?' You wouldn't say, 'Well, gee what are you having? And how are you gonna cook it?'"

The actor immediately accepted the offer, but not just because he enjoys Darabont's company. "It's always exciting material," says DeMunn. "He always brings quality people together and nice people at the same time; people that are pleasant to be around. Plus, we're friends. There's a wonderful communication

EPISODE 3: "TELL IT TO THE FROGS"

Teleplay by Charles H. Eglee & Jack LoGiudice and Frank Darabont
Story by Charles H. Eglee & Jack LoGiudice
Directed by Gwyneth Horder-Payton

CARL: Think about it, Mom. Everything that's happened to him so far.
Nothing's killed him yet.

SYNOPSIS: As Merle struggles to get free of his handcuffs on a roof that could be overrun by the undead at any moment, the other survivors return to camp. Everyone is glad for their safe return, but nothing compares to the emotional reunion when Rick discovers that Lori and Carl are among the group. Shane is also happy to see his friend alive, but worries what it means for his budding relationship with Lori.

The group sits around a low campfire listening to Rick share his tale of waking in the abandoned hospital. Lori explains that she was told the patients were going to be

evacuated to Atlanta. Rick understands the situation and harbors no blame for her or Shane. He has nothing but gratitude for his friend's actions that protected his family.

Another camper, Ed Peletier, adds a log to the fire, but Shane warns him to keep the flame low to avoid unwanted attention. Shane has fallen into a leadership role at the camp, and he removes the log while checking on Ed's wife and daughter, Carol and Sophia.

The Grimes family retires to their tent, where Lori apologizes without explaining the full depth of her regrets. Rick sees the situation as a second chance to fix the things that had gone wrong in their marriage, and Lori returns his wedding ring. They make love in their tent, while Shane is alone out in the rain keeping watch on the camp.

The next morning Glenn's stolen car is stripped for fuel and parts as the survivors go about their chores. Rick can't stop thinking about Merle and wants to go back to save him, but Carl and Sophia's screams put an end to his conversation with Lori on the matter. The kids came across a Walker in the woods devouring a dead deer. It's

CONTINUED

the first creature that's come this far outside the city. The men destroy the Walker that was making a meal out of Daryl Dixon's fresh kill.

Daryl doesn't take the news about his brother well. T-Dog accepts responsibility for what happened, and he explains that he chained the door to the roof shut behind him and that Merle could still be alive. Daryl demands that they tell him where his brother is, but Lori interrupts to say that won't be necessary. She looks to her husband who informs everyone that he is going back.

Shane tries to convince Rick to stay and protect the camp, but Merle isn't the only reason to return. Rick's gun bag is sitting on an Atlanta street, filled with weapons, ammunition, and the walkie-talkie. Without that, he can't warn Morgan and Duane away from Atlanta. Rick and Daryl head back into the city with T-Dog and Glenn to get the guns and find Merle.

Shane tries to talk to Lori about their situation, but she shuts him down, blaming him for lying to her about Rick's death. When they see Ed strike his wife, Shane jumps to the woman's defense, beating Ed badly as he takes out all his frustrations on the man.

In Atlanta, Merle is no longer on the roof where he was last seen. All that remains are the handcuffs, a hacksaw, and Merle's hand.

thing that can happen with someone that you've worked with more than once, where you really don't need to finish the whole sentence. He can say something to me and I get it right away, and back to him as well. It works both ways."

Just because the executive producer wanted to hire actors he'd worked with before did not necessarily mean they got the part. AMC, like any network, had final casting approval over the series. To help convince the network that DeMunn should play the part of Dale, Bialy and Thomas broke out their art supplies. "We knew that Frank wanted Jeffrey DeMunn for the role," Bialy says. "And he looked so much like the character in the graphic novel that we found pictures of Jeffrey and we put them next to pictures from the novel and we sent the whole board over to AMC to show them how great he looked." They wound up doing this with some of the other actors as well after they found that, purely by coincidence, a number of their dream cast members bore eerie similarities to the comic characters.

Another benefit of Darabont working with his regular stable of talent is that these people have gotten to know one another and are comfortable working together as well. Though actors are hired to create relationships even when they are working alongside total strangers, it was likely beneficial that DeMunn had worked with Holden before, considering the relationship that develops between Dale and Andrea in the comics. We see hints of that relationship forming in the first season of the series. It's an important element for both of the characters, particularly in light of the death of Andrea's sister, Amy, as played by Emma Bell.

Although every character in the series has experienced loss, both Dale and Andrea are touched so personally by that death in particular that they can find comfort in one another.

In approaching Dale's friendship with these two younger women—Andrea and Amy—DeMunn took his motivation from the script page, as well as the comic book page. In the comic, when Dale meets the two young women, he is still mourning the loss of his wife. "I took my cue from the fact that he had lost his lifelong friend," DeMunn said. "He had lost the person that he was absolutely happy with and had been together with for many, many years. When she was taken away, in a very real sense, his life ended. Then due to the circumstances that they were involved in, and due to the fact that he was put in a position of being able to help two people, it started him back alive again."

But Dale was not untouched by the new world order. "That was pretty much my starting point," DeMunn continues. "These were the two people that brought me back to the world again and yet brought [me] back with a big difference in that I don't feel like Dale has anything to lose. He lived his life, and his life ended. And now, in a way, it gives him a certain amount of courage and fearlessness. Because, 'What are you gonna do? You gonna kill me? You gonna take my wife away?' The worst has happened to him, and he survived and he's still standing and I think it's made him stronger."

The Dale–Andrea–Amy trio was built off the pages of the comic book and stayed fairly true to the source material. There is a bit more of an age difference between Andrea and Amy

ABOVE: A brief implication in a line of Carol's dialogue from page 13 of issue no. 5 served as the inspiration for her abusive husband, Ed, and their first-season story line.

on-screen and Dale's wife dies under different circumstances in the comic, but the emotional beats are similar for the characters.

In another case, a story line and character that were original to the television series also found their starting point on the comic page. Carol and Sophia are integral characters in the comic book. Although Melissa McBride does not physically match the comic character as closely as many of her costars do, Carol of the TV series has many emotional similarities with her original version.

Carol's husband is already dead by the time we meet her in the comic. He was another victim of the undead uprising. But in issue no. 5, there is a brief reference to some possible darkness in their relationship. It is never discussed, nor expanded on in the book, but Darabont and the other TV writers took that nugget and grew it into a character, bringing her husband, Ed,

into the story and giving Carol more emotional impact by having her experience his death in front of the viewing audience.

"Melissa McBride is a terrific actress," says Hurd. "She's someone that Frank worked with previously on *The Mist*. So he knew that in crafting her character and expanding from the comic book, he could really give her some very weighty, dramatic moments, because she was the kind of actress that could pull it off. There's no question she was an abused wife. She was doing everything she could to protect her daughter. She has a quiet strength. You see in the scene where Shane starts to really beat up Ed, that conflict that abused women have. You want it to stop, but it's become so familiar."

Rounding out the characters from the comic, the producers found yet another actor who was, coincidentally, a perfect match for his comic counterpart. The casting directors once

ABOVE: Jim's story in the TV series closely mirrors that of his comic counterpart.

again created an art project to convince AMC that Andrew Rothenberg was the perfect choice for the role of Jim, the man haunted by the loss of his family. It was another story line lifted straight from the page, although it was expanded with Jim's premonitory dream that motivated him to start digging graves.

The addition of characters like the Morales family, Jacqui, and T-Dog would not only add to the diversity of the cast, but bring new dynamics to the relationships with which readers were already familiar. Dr. Jenner (Noah Emmerich), the "Vatos" gang, and the senior citizens added fresh story lines for the writers to explore. At the same time, there was a trimming of the cast of characters from the comic. Allen, Donna, and their twins, Billy and Ben, would be excised from the series, although there's always a chance that they could come in at a later time.

"From the very beginning," Hurd explains, "Frank and Robert agreed that we could populate the series with characters from the comic book and characters that didn't exist in the comic book, as well as not using some characters that he had appear in the comic book. It really was about 'Who are the people that make this group the most interesting?' You don't just create a character for the sake of numbers. It really is 'What do they bring to this community?'"

Two of the most intriguing new characters were the brothers Merle and Daryl Dixon. Merle's subplot was the first major departure from the established comic story line. His disappearance at the end of episode 3 also left the door open for future stories. Many fans of the comic suspect that Merle could later return in the role of the villainous Governor from the comics, though Darabont has signaled that is unlikely—while, at the same time, cryptically hinting that it could be a possibility.

Merle's brother Daryl, played by Norman Reedus, seems to be cut from the same cloth, but with a somewhat softer, gentler side as well. "I've loved discovering what an intriguing character Daryl is," says Darabont. "He's a guy that I really didn't expect to like. He's not necessarily a guy I'd want to hang out with, but I can see that for all his messed-up mind-set in certain ways, he's a guy who has sort of a basic code of honor. He's got some issues he's got to work through certainly, but I like this guy. He actually winds up as an 'if you play square with him he'll play square with you' kind of a character. That, I didn't expect. And I like it."

Another new character who brought much to the series was Jeryl Prescott's Jacqui. Though Jacqui never played a focal role in the episodes until the very end of season one, the character quickly established herself as a favorite among viewers and the production unit as well. This made it hard for the writers to fulfill her primary purpose. "Jacqui, as a character, was invented literally so I'd have somebody to stay with Jenner at the end," explains Darabont. "And then we cast Jeryl. And Jeryl comes along and, even with a minimal amount of screen time, becomes a character that we love. She's a gorgeously skilled actress."

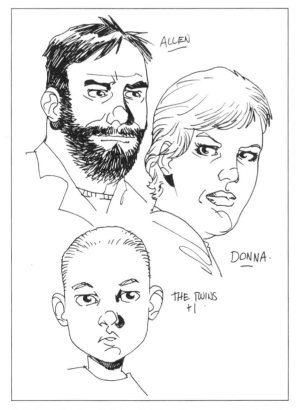

ABOVE: The tragic tale of Allen, Donna, and their twin boys, Billy and Ben, was one of the first casualties of adapting the comic book to the TV series.

Darabont recalls that he was feeling pressure both from his coworkers and from himself when it came time to have Jacqui remain behind. "Nobody wanted to say good-bye to Jeryl," Darabont admits. "I didn't want to say good-bye to Jeryl. I didn't even really get the chance to work with her on the set, but she was giving such a great performance I thought, 'Oh man, my guilt level is rising as we're getting to that script.' I'm thinking, 'Maybe there's a way not to do it.' And then I thought, 'No, that's just a cop-out if I don't.' I mean, there's a reason that character was there. Ultimately, everything has to serve the greater story."

Darabont believes that it would have been a hollow letdown if it had only been Dr. Jenner sitting in the room as the CDC self-destructed, and ultimately, the scene was worth the tough decision. "Now, it's something that you won't ever be able to pry out of your mind," he says. "Or at least I won't. Particularly the level of grace and dignity with which Jeryl played it makes it extremely memorable to me. That moment where they clasp hands, she and Jenner. And Noah Emmerich was also so great."

From here on out, it's only going to get harder for Darabont. If the writers continue to follow the path of *The Walking Dead* comic series, Jacqui's will be far from the last death. Rick Grimes will continue to lose friends and meet new people. New cast members will join the series, filling out the roles that fans of the comic books have come to love. Maybe there will be entirely new characters as well. For Rick and the other survivors, the journey has just begun.

FIVE

ADAPTING THE VISUAL STYLE OF *THE WALKING DEAD*

"Every once in a while we turned to one of the AMC executives and said, 'You know we're actually making a movie? You know that?' . . . And they'd go, 'Yeah, we pretty much figured that.' We approached every day like we were making a movie, and whatever we needed to do to have that sense of scale and quality was what we were going to do, albeit within the context of shooting very, very quickly."

—Frank Darabont

In developing *The Walking Dead* for television, the executive producers pulled together their crew of artists and technicians from the movie world, in which they have spent the greater part of their careers. Not only does Frank Darabont enjoy working with a core group of actors, but he also brings many of his crew members along with him from project to project. They are intensely loyal and immensely talented—necessary qualities to create a TV show that could match the scope of the comic, as well the vision of the man bringing it to television.

For the pilot episode, the producers called on the talents of David Tattersall as director of photography to help Darabont establish the visual tone of the series. The D.P. is effectively

ABOVE: Long shots like this one emphasized the solitude Rick faced on the open road.

the director's right-hand person on set, in charge of the lighting and camera operation. Tattersall, who has worked in Hollywood for decades on films such as *Star Wars:* Episodes I–III and Darabont's *The Green Mile* and *The Majestic*, jumped at the chance to work with the director again. "Frank is a real-deal filmmaker," says Tattersall. "He's a real fan of classic, cinematic storytelling. He doesn't leave much to chance. It's all very well organized and very well prepped, and he loves cinematography. He loves to talk about it; he loves to work with the camera. He talks about the dance the camera does with the actors. It's all part of having fun manipulating the audience through blocking the action, photographic coverage, and, ultimately, the editing. It's a real pleasure working with Frank."

To shape his vision for the television pilot, Darabont naturally looked to the source material as his inspiration. "I love the starkness and the simplicity of both the Moore and the Adlard artwork in the comic book," he says. "In a way, it has the starkness and simplicity of *Night of the Living Dead....* That lovely sort of

ABOVE: The zombie hordes that fill the pages of the comic book, like in this double page spread from issue no. 59, are just one element of the comic that the production team looked forward to re-creating.

OPPOSITE: Charlie Adlard's art style relies heavily on the use of black in the "coloring" of the pages, bringing a darkness to the comic books that is not easily matched in the TV series, which more often films in daylight.

PREVIOUS SPREAD: Shots of the lone sheriff's deputy were a recurring image in the series pilot.

stark art, but with tremendously accomplished flourishes. The art is never fussy, but it can be tremendously effecting. Indeed, we've tried to take as much inspiration from the designs that these gentlemen have provided us and realized them on-screen."

"The graphic novels are kind of like a rather exotic storyboard," Tattersall notes. "Some of the more iconic images we did reproduce pretty accurately." Storyboards aren't always used in television series, simply because the tighter schedules afford no time in which to create them. Having an already-established visual guide helped, within the confines of television, to bring a larger-scale, filmic quality to the series.

"Frank really wanted to shoot this like a feature film and not be forced into cramming a complicated sequence into a short space of time," Tattersall explains. "He wanted to stretch out the quiet moments. I think that helps give that expansive, cinematic feeling. The coverage was mostly two cameras; occasionally it was three. We very rarely just grabbed anything. We had the luxury of a couple of weeks of prep, and with that, Frank would often drive out to the known locations, walking through and chatting through, so we did really know what we were getting into. . . . One of the styles we really tried to keep was a moody, drifting, lingering camera that I think helped the spooky atmosphere. We never went for a handheld; it was never jittery or frenetic."

In adapting the black-and-white comic for the screen, Darabont and Tattersall agreed that

ABOVE: As the actors make their way through dangerous streets, tension is enhanced through the use of silent, lingering shots.

the use of Super 16mm film would mimic the feel of the comic art. David Boyd, who took over as D.P. for episodes 2 through 6, wholeheartedly agrees with the choice, as he too looked to the comic for guidance. "Everything about the graphic novel influenced what I did with the photography on *The Walking Dead*," says Boyd. "I admire all the choices that went into the books: black and white; everyone squeezed vertically; divergent aspect ratios to the frames. It was important to me to absorb first the emotions conveyed by the books, and then assign the tools I have available to the cinematography so that my work would do as much justice as possible to the printed works. I would love to see the project photographed in black and white. Given that color photography is a requirement, our choice to shoot *The Walking Dead* on 16mm film—with its distinctive grain structure and resolution—does a lot, I think, to approximate the raw honesty of the books."

Both directors of photography agree that shooting on Super 16, and particularly the light and agile cameras used for filming, have benefited the production. "I haven't seen a crew this happy with the equipment in a real long time," Boyd notes. "Setup time between shots, or even takes, is superfast. There's no train behind it like there is with the digital cameras. I'd estimate saving two hours easily every production day shooting 16mm film on this particular show. This choice of camera system allows us to put most of our efforts into the story and the cast performances, which are, after all, why we're all into the show."

One of the things that sets *The Walking Dead* apart from traditional zombie movies is that much of the action takes place in daylight. So the directors and cinematographers are forced to set a mood without using darkness and shadow, the traditional tricks of the trade. It has become a challenge that Boyd proudly accepts. "My heart soars any time a filming strategy goes its own way," he says. "I love the idea that, with zombies afoot, the day is scary also. It's great to turn the traditional on its head."

Having worked on a number of horror films in the eighties, like *Re-Animator* and *From Beyond*, Boyd is quite familiar with capturing that horror "vibe," whether filming by day or night. "It comes with a choice of angle or height," he says. "Lingering on some one thing perhaps a little too long. We keep the cameras a touch nervous all the time, like scuba divers at night. We are just a few humans, after all, in a sea of scary beings. And we're all on the run."

Those cameras would be trained on many locations and sets that were fully realized pages of the comic book created by a talented team of production artists, many of whom have also worked with Darabont before. The sets for the first three episodes were crafted under the direction of Production Designer Greg Melton, who has worked on series as diverse as *Private Practice* and *Tales from the Crypt*, and who has been friends with Darabont since they were teens.

Starting on the pilot, Melton was handed an episode that stuck almost religiously to the source material, which provided him with the same storyboard used by the directors of photography. The production designer felt the best way to achieve the proper look was to refer to what he'd been given. "We're very fortunate to

THE MUSIC BEHIND
THE MAIN TITLE SEQUENCE

ABOVE: The imagery of the main title sequence emphasizes the desolation of the postapocalyptic world, underscored by the growing intensity of the music playing beneath it.

The main title sequence of a TV series functions as more than a means of revealing the names of the actors in the show and the producers behind its creation. It briefly and perfectly encapsulates the tone of the series in a visual and aural montage. Fewer and fewer shows have extended title sequences these days, preferring to go right into the action to avoid the risk of losing an inattentive audience. But the haunting opening of *The Walking Dead* is very much an integral part of pulling the viewers into the show's postapocalyptic setting.

The visuals of the main titles, which were designed by Kyle Cooper at Prologue Films, open by documenting the empty streets of Atlanta, devoid of human life. This produces an eerie tone and creates a powerful backdrop upon which to build. Layered over these desolate scenes are photographs of the characters that appear worn and grimy, as if they were salvaged from antiquated wreckage. The titles, which also use scenes from the show, intricate editing, stock footage, and animated or heavily manipulated second-unit photography, foreshadow the tale's focus on individuals struggling to maintain a sense of humanity after the zombie apocalypse.

Underneath those visuals plays the hauntingly repetitive score composed by Bear McCreary, who has worked on other notable genre shows including *Terminator: The Sarah Connor Chronicles* and *Battlestar Galactica*. "My goal in the main title sequence was to create a scene that captured the tone of the series," explains McCreary. "In fact, ironically, the main title sequence is more energetic than a lot of the music I write for the series. It's sort of a dichotomy that we're creating where the images that you're seeing are very static and the music that you're hearing is very exciting. It's the kind of music that *could* go under a very quickly cut, energetic action scene." In fact, that music was designed to begin under the action of the episode teaser, pulling the audience into the main title sequence before the images even start to roll.

McCreary not only used the music to set the tone for the show, but also to establish the instrumentation that would underscore the episodes. "What you hear is a very small string orchestra of six or eight players," he says. "And you hear the southern Georgian blues instrumentation as well. You hear electric guitar, electric bass, and you hear Autoharps and dulcimer and a little electric banjo. These are the instruments that really define the score. You just get a little taste of them. It's like the main titles give you a little taste of everything that the score is built from. It's the musical DNA of the score."

The other goal was to create a memorable theme that stays with the viewer. "The entire theme is based on a one-eighth-note pattern," says McCreary. "It just repeats over and over and over again. In the course of a thirty-second main title, you hear it over a dozen times, so it really gets stuck in your head, and it becomes this catchy little earworm that burrows into your brain. But it's very subtle. I didn't want it to feel like a theme song, but it is infectiously catchy. Kind of like a zombie disease, I guess."

have a visual narrative to draw upon in designing *The Walking Dead*," says Melton. "You are able to see the entire arc of the show, and of course, we found ourselves inspired to use some key

ABOVE: The production art department works very closely with the visual effects team to determine when sets may need computer-aided enhancements. The goal is to dress everything on location without the additional cost of CGI. The gas station set is one of the earlier sets considered for CGI, but it was eventually created entirely through practical set dressing on location.

images. First and foremost is Rick's approach to the skyline of Atlanta. That was such an iconic panel from the comic book that it had a great influence over my work."

That comic book template would be less necessary by the middle of the short season, as the TV story diverged from what was on the page. At the same time, Alex Hajdu moved up from the art director position to take over as production designer in episode 4. The new settings in that episode gave him some freedom to explore, which was his preferred take on adapting the source material. "I deliberately did not use the comic," he explains. "I did not want to copy or be derivative. We tried to keep the spirit of the world created in the comic, and use it as a taking-off point. I think the only thing I took from it was the graphic use of negative space, and the technique of simplifying what was in the frame, keeping it uncluttered."

He did stay true to the tone of the comic, though, noting that the realism of live-action television would ground the already gritty and realistic artwork even more dramatically. "The intention was to keep it real," Hajdu explains. "Real people in real places doing real things. This was about people surviving in a world that's broken down and is dangerous to live in. It's really more like a war movie. It just happens to be zombies instead of the Nazis. . . . I tried not to make it stylized in any overt way."

The survivalist motif is evident in the pilot episode, as Rick Grimes pulls his police cruiser in beside burned-out and abandoned vehicles surrounding a gas station. The languid manner

ABOVE: Google's SketchUp program, in conjunction with Google Maps, aided the production in laying out the design for a location in advance, saving time that would have been spent dressing the scene.

in which the vehicle approaches the scene and Rick takes in the devastation tells us the emergency is over. There is nothing the law can do here. It visually sets the tone for life in this postapocalyptic world.

"Total isolation was the approach to the gas station," explains Melton. "We looked all over greater Atlanta for a highway with a lone gas station. There had to be no other buildings in sight. It was the end of the line for lots of refugees. Rick is crossing large areas of the state with no one in sight, and then he wanders into this zombie-infested gas station."

Although the series is set in a world where modern technology rarely functions, that same equipment was invaluable to the production

team. Since the pilot was on such a tight filming schedule, the art department did as much pre-production work as possible so they would be ready to go in and shoot on the day of filming.

In preparing for dressing the gas station set before they were physically at the location, the design team used Google Earth, in conjunction with the SketchUp design program, for 3-D modeling. This allowed them to digitally add cars in a scale representation taken from a satellite view of the gas station to find out how many vehicles they would need and what composition would be best. On the day of shooting, it was only a matter of positioning the abandoned vehicles according to their predetermined layout, map literally in hand. "The gas

EPISODE 4: "VATOS"

Written by Robert Kirkman
Directed by Johan Renck

SHANE:...Jim, nobody's gonna hurt you, you hear me? Shhh. Jim. Hey.
Nobody is gonna hurt you.

JIM: That's a lie. It's the biggest lie there is. I told that to my wife
and my two boys. I said it a hundred times. It didn't matter. They came out
of nowhere. There were dozens of them. They just pulled 'em right out of
my hand. You know, the only reason I got away was 'cause the dead were
too busy eating my family.

SYNOPSIS: Andrea and Amy share memories of their father while fishing in the quarry,
which only makes the two very different sisters miss their parents more. Meanwhile,
high above them, Jim is exhaustively digging holes in the one-hundred-degree heat.
Dale is concerned by his friend's inexplicable behavior and informs the other campers, but Jim turns violent when the group tries to stop him.

In the city, Daryl collects his brother's hand, and he, Rick, T-Dog, and Glenn set off in search of Merle. They follow his blood into a building, where they find evidence that Merle cauterized the wound and escaped. With the trail cold, they turn their attention to the gun bag in the street, in spite of Daryl insisting that they keep on the search. Glenn comes up with a plan to get the guns, but it is dependent on him venturing out onto the Geek-filled streets on his own while the other men wait in two different alleyways to provide cover. As Glenn goes for the guns, Daryl comes across a kid in his alley who starts screaming for help. Two other guys pull up to the alley in a car and start beating on Daryl when they see him on top of their friend. When Glenn returns to the alley, the new arrivals attack him and pull him into a car. Rick, Daryl, and T-Dog still have the guns and the screaming kid, but they've lost Glenn.

Their new captive, Miguel, takes Rick, T-Dog, and Daryl to see his "boss," Guillermo. With guns drawn, Rick offers a trade of Miguel for Glenn, but Guillermo

CONTINUED

also wants the guns. The two groups part so Rick can consider their next move. Daryl suggests that they shouldn't risk their lives for Glenn, but Rick feels indebted to the pizza delivery guy who got him out of the tank.

A second meeting doesn't go any better than the first, until an elderly woman wanders into the showdown. The gang is protecting the residents of a retirement home who were left behind when the staff fled. Seeing the situation differently now, Rick splits the guns and ammunition with the gang members and leaves with Glenn. When they get to the spot where they left the truck, they find that it's gone and assume that Merle took it. They now have to make the long return trip to the campsite on foot.

Jim's actions are blamed on heatstroke, but the others tie him to a tree until they can be reassured that he is better. Jim tries to make amends, but he can't explain his actions beyond saying that the idea to dig the holes came to him in a dream.

That night, the campers settle in around the fire with a calmer Jim freed from his restraints. During their quiet moment, the camp is overwhelmed by the undead. Rick and his group return in the midst of the attack, too late to save everyone. Amy, Ed, and several other campers are killed in the attack.

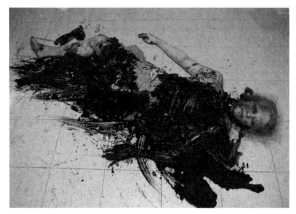

ABOVE: The sights to which Rick wakes in the hospital were carefully planned to both mimic the comic book and bring a deeper visual horror through the use of makeup effects, lighting, and the choice of film stock to give a stylistic look to the gore-filled halls.

station set was a huge dress for us, but we got it installed and dressed in one day with no CGI enhancement," Melton adds with pride. "It was entirely practical."

While the opening scenes on that desolate Georgia road were filmed entirely live with no computer enhancement, that would not be true of the overall series. *The Walking Dead* is an impressive example of the seamless use of computer-generated effects to add to the visuals of series television. If *The Walking Dead* had been produced fifteen years ago, it would be a completely different show, technically speaking, relying on glass paintings to physically augment the existing sets. This would have limited what the production crew could accomplish in establishing the world of the show, and likely been noticeable to the audience at home.

When the episode flashed back to Rick's hometown, a combination of practical locations mixed with CGI-enhanced exteriors created the hospital where Rick was ushered into this new, ever-worsening reality. "The hospital location was one of my favorite sets to create," says Melton. "It was a closed rehab center with lots of corridors and rooms available to us. We were able to use bits and pieces of the existing space to create Rick's slow descent into the madness of his new world."

The storytelling aspect of the set design was important, as there were no people around to explain to Rick what had happened. He and the audience have to piece it together from the visuals. "It really became about art-directing these areas where summary executions took place or there were running gun battles and spots where grenades went off," Melton continues. "The idea was that it would just go from bad to worse with every step Rick took. It was tricky, because you don't want to make it cartoony or over the top. It had to have realism. That was important in every element of the show. There needed to be a realistic world at the core so we could let the surreal horror spin out of it."

Tattersall added to the visual misery with lighting effects to set the mood in the hospital corridors. "We had a bit of fun with that with the emergency fluorescent light, adding a bit of

ABOVE: The scene of Rick descending the staircase is a traditional misdirection horror trope. The audience suffers through a suspense-filled walk in the dark expecting an attack only to experience a communal sigh of relief as Rick escapes into the bright light of day.

flickering light here and there," he says. "I think it worked really well for the half-eaten body in the corridor." The horrific visual of this body was further enhanced by the choice of the Super 16 film and the developing process. "The slight desaturation was a conscious effort to take away from the bright red," he continues, "and also the grain texture helped bring everything together." The blood came across as more muted on film than in real life, which toned down some of the gore, but still kept the horrific visuals created by Greg Nicotero's makeup team.

As Rick walks through the halls witnessing horror after horror, he comes to the doors marked DON'T OPEN DEAD INSIDE, and he has the first real inkling that not only has something terrifying taken place, but the threat persists. This ratchets up the tension and his need to flee, bringing him into a scene straight out of a traditional horror movie. An action as simple as walking down a staircase is made more suspenseful when the only visible light source comes from the matches that Rick carries with him.

"That was a tricky and fairly ambitious idea going into it; a single match–open light source," says Tattersall. "We used a 25-watt projector bulb that the actor actually held himself, in his hand. Our gaffer made a little aluminum cup shaped to fit inside the palm of his hand. There was a little wire that went to a battery with a radio-controlled flicker dimmer—which I think was the first time it's ever been used. It would flicker the bulb to mimic a match. Because it was so close to where the match was that he was holding, it created a pretty effective single shadow and point source with enough lumens for the film to capture it. We were all pretty happy with the way that came out."

When Rick exits the stairwell, the horror in the hospital corridors dims in comparison, as the audience gets the first real glimpse of the intensive level of work the visual effects team would do in creating the world of *The Walking Dead*. "The exterior hospital was conceived and executed by using practical sets and enhancing them with CGI," explains Melton. "The back of the location gave us some extra areas for Rick to

ABOVE: Nightmarish visions await Rick outside the hospital. This was the first major set to combine a practical location with makeup-effect sculpted bodies and CGI enhancements to add to the scope of the devastation.

discover the building horror so that his view of the situation continued to get worse and worse until he reached the upper parking lot, [where] we created a MASH unit. There was basically one real helicopter at the location, and then CGI set extensions were added to give it all the scope."

Creating the hospital exterior required detailed conversations between Darabont and his production team. "The initial give-and-take was how to balance what we were going to have practically, in terms of bodies, versus what we were going to have to digitally enhance," explains Jason Sperling. "The hospital's a really cool example of how production design, Greg Nicotero's special effects work, and our work kind of seamlessly blend together. The production design had all

of these great little hints of the chaos and the destruction that had come before Rick seeing this tableau of a military encampment abandoned and bodies everywhere."

Adding a human toll to the devastation, Nicotero provided fifty dummy bodies partially covered by sheets to fill the loading dock. "The idea is, if the zombie apocalypse has happened, there's going to be a lot of bodies lying around," he says. "It's not going to be clean streets." The visual effects team even went in and digitally added flies to some of the decaying bodies in the final scene. But to really sell the horror, they were going to need even more bodies, which were simply not practical for the makeup team to create.

Instead, the visual effects team took those fifty bodies and digitally cloned them into *five hundred* bodies, making up rows and rows of corpses in the loading dock. They also filled trucks and every available space with the CGI bodies—but the devastation did not end there.

Rick climbs a hill to see the abandoned military encampment that was left after what looked to be a small war. What actor Andrew Lincoln walked through on the day of filming was nothing like what the audience saw when the episode aired. "The only thing that was there was the actual helicopter body," says Sperling. "Not even the propellers or the rotors or anything like that." Every other element of that scene was added digitally, from the helicopter parts to the second helicopter, Humvees, tents, and the devastation, to the building in the background. "That scene is a really cool example of just how all those three different departments seamlessly work together to create a sense that a lot of chaos had happened in that place, but all these little moments and stories of what that chaos was are still left to the imagination."

Although Sperling and his boss, Sam Nicholson, take noticeable pride in the achievements of their department, they are both quick to note that the visual effects follow the lead of the production and makeup design; they do not establish the look. Nicholson explains, "The general rule is, do everything you can real, and when money runs out, VFX extends it. If you can do fifty bodies, great. If you can do a hundred, even better. But our limit was about fifty that would look great, so Greg could concentrate

on fewer quantity and better quality, and then we could clone it."

Nicholson compares the process to audio sampling, but on a visual level. "We visually sample on set," he says. "So we shoot extensively all of the details: the bodies, the faces, every single zombie, every single element. Whether it's broken concrete or whatever, we sample it. We still-photograph in high definition, and then

ABOVE: The visual effects team rendered the upper parking lot location by adding in the entire base camp piece by piece, building off the partial helicopter at the location.

THE CAMP ATTACK

ABOVE: Re-creating the camp attack in issue no. 5 was an important moment in the TV series, requiring a tremendous amount of collaboration to fit the scenes into the production schedule.

"We were up there on that little ridgeline when vans arrived and this crowd of forty-five or fifty silent zombies came walking up the little dirt road. We all sort of parted—went to one side and the other—and let them through. They didn't say a word. I suppose they'd been told just to go up there, keep quiet, and wait to be told what to do. We needed that kind of discipline over all of us to get through a night like that. But it was weird, standing there watching these people as they were looking at us."

—Jeffrey DeMunn

SYNOPSIS: "Vatos" takes a dramatic turn away from the story line established in *The Walking Dead* comic books. The plot is set up to lead the viewers to make assumptions about the gang that allowed the writers to have a surprise reveal when the gang's true motivation comes to light. That twist was particularly necessary in adding a surprise element to an episode that was going to end with a very important moment that readers of the comic book were probably expecting, if not greatly anticipating.

The nighttime campsite attack is an important pivot in both the comic and the television series: It is the first time that established characters die. The fact that it starts while Rick and his group are away has additional repercussions in the Rick–Shane dynamic in the series. Also, for practical reasons, it trims the cast of the nonspeaking survivors so that a smaller group can take the caravan on to their next destination in the following episode.

A massive amount of coordination was necessary on the night of filming to get the main action down. "Cast and crew just went for it that night," says D.P. David Boyd. "The photographic challenge lay in reconciling my desire to shoot all directions at the same time and keeping the considerable lighting equipment invisible. I cleared land far away above the camp to accept six or eight firestarter maxi-brutes (big, punchy lights), and I hung ambient fill overhead nearby. I wanted this scene in particular to feel raw and unproduced. I wanted everyone's shadows all over everyone else—chaos, in Greek terms. I felt if we put faith in filming what happened, rather than shooting what we want to have happen, we would best get the zombie onslaught across emotionally. The rest is making sure that each dramatic moment and connection between the characters is on film as written. You can imagine what a free-for-all it was that night."

Part of that well-planned free-for-all involved having Key Special Makeup Effects Supervisor Greg Nicotero direct the pickup shots. These brief, inserted close-up moments of the attack would enhance the action of the main shoot. Since Nicotero knew better than anyone what his makeup effects could do to create the kind of carnage the attack called for, it was only natural to consider the role a part of his consulting producer title. "One of the things Frank and I talked about for that scene is that we need to feel the menace and the threat," he says. "Zombies can't just walk into camp and stagger around. We need to see people taken down. We need to see people bitten. We need to see Morales with a baseball bat splattering somebody's head. You have to play up the idea that this is a genuine threat and people are dying."

ABOVE: After principal photography wrapped on the camp attack scenes, three additional hours of pickup shots were filmed using a select group of extras for close-up kills.

CONTINUED

ABOVE: Greg Nicotero worked closely with Emma Bell to perfect the re-creation of Amy's death from issue no. 5, page 14. The run-through they filmed for Darabont convinced Nicotero that he should play the role of the zombie for the important scene.

CONTINUED

Frank Darabont told Nicotero to shoot what he needed in the pickups, under the constraints of having only three hours to film it. "We made up eight zombies, and we shot six little vignettes," Nicotero explains. "One shot we'd bring two in the front and six in the back, and the next shot we'd bring another two up front and move those two around. We just stacked it so it just felt like there were dozens of zombies in those shots, and it was the same eight, just moved around."

One of the zombies Nicotero used for the close-up attacks had been a personal favorite of his since they first met in zombie school. The actor, Travis Carpenter, was exactly what Nicotero wanted to embody the zombie physique, and he'd asked the actor if he'd ever consider doing his scene with his shirt off. "At the beginning," he explains, "I wanted to do a couple of zombies that really looked emaciated and we could put bites on them." The actor was not only game, he went so far as to remove his shirt right there and suck in his gut to show the designer just what kind of special effect his body could create on its own. The action made his slim frame almost concave in the stomach, emphasizing his rib cage to almost unnatural proportions.

ABOVE: Special effects makeup artist Kevin Wasner works on zombie extra Travis Carpenter, who possessed a particular talent that helped provide the emaciated effect the makeup team desired.

Two months later, on the night of shooting the zombie attack, Carpenter reminded the makeup effects supervisor of their earlier conversation, which led to him being the standout zombie of the night. "Frank thought that character was so memorable," Nicotero adds. "He called and said, 'Do you have more footage of him?' I said, 'I had three hours to shoot everything. I wish I had more footage.'"

Nicotero also spent some time rehearsing with Emma Bell for the climactic moment when Amy is bitten and killed by a zombie. "Emma and I had actually set the camera up outside the makeup trailer and shot her whole death sequence and cut it together," he explains, referring to their rehearsals preceding the night shoot. "I sent it to Frank and showed it to the director and said, 'Here's the blocking. Here's where we should put the camera.' That way he could not only maximize the performance, but determine where the blood tube could be placed so that it would be hidden from the camera when it started shooting out blood."

It was important for Nicotero to know exactly where the bite would be placed on the actress during the filming because the blood effects had to match perfectly, or else the entire moment wouldn't work. The makeup specialist has had a great deal of experience on projects in which a featured extra would be so in the moment when the director yelled *action* that he would get carried away and forget the specifics. "Even a miss of mere inches could throw off the effect," Nicotero notes. "They have to hit the mark and also be cognizant of where the camera is so that they don't block the gag, that the gag pays off, that the actors get all their motivation and everything."

Since it was such a key moment in the series, it was decided that Nicotero himself would play the zombie who kills Amy, making this his second zombie cameo in the series (earlier, he had played a zombie dining on a dead deer). "Emma and I really spent time working through it," he explains. "It was the first character that we see bitten by a zombie in the first season, so it was really important that the choreography worked and that the gags worked."

Nicotero gets a lot of grief from friends who think he does this just because he likes to play zombies. While the self-proclaimed geek certainly doesn't disagree, that's not his sole motivation. "There is a purpose behind me doing it," he says. "And the purpose is that I know exactly how to choreograph it to make it work right, and it worked really well."

we clone it, manipulate it, texture-wrap it, put it on 3-D objects, and literally create clones of the zombies or the bodies or the whatever. Some things have to be created, like say, the helicopter or the Humvees that are up in the military camp. Those are complete 3-D models from scratch, but still the textures on them are derived from the real helicopter. We were very proud that when we put our virtual helicopter next to the real helicopter that was there, they are indistinguishable. So if you get it to that point, then you know you've done it correctly."

Coming from the hospital, Rick has his first brief, but meaningful, encounter with a walker before returning to his home in search of his wife and son. Finding the real places that would serve as Rick's personal landmarks took more than just choosing a house or a workplace. These locations commented on his character and the small town in which he lived. He's not some big action-hero military expert—he's a small-town sheriff's deputy.

Location Manager Mike Riley found a home in the Grant Park section of Atlanta that matched the aesthetic Melton had in mind. "It was an abandoned house that was up for sale," says Melton. "It was boarded up and missing all the windows and doors, but it had the look and layout we were after. We went to the trouble of fixing it up, building new windows

ABOVE: The Grimes family home, located in Kentucky in the story, was only minutes from the downtown Atlanta filming locations.

and doors and entirely painting the interior. We then proceeded to dress it for the Grimes family, but left behind the evidence of a quick exit with scrapbooks and pictures missing throughout the house."

For the police station, the search wasn't exactly exhaustive: The location was right in their own backyard. "As I was scouting, the image of the police station in the comic book was hard to shake," says Melton. "The location we found ended up being this little red brick building right next door to the production office that had the same feel as the comic book." That comic book proved indispensable for Melton when planning every set in the pilot. "It was like having a storyboard from beginning to end."

Whether in residential neighborhoods or, later, in the streets of downtown Atlanta, the production team not only had to dress sets to comment on the characters, but also tell the story of this postapocalyptic world. "Fortunately for

ABOVE: For the pilot episode's police station, the production team looked to the first panel on page 17 of issue no. 1 for inspiration. They found the perfect building right beside the production office.

us, the apocalypse had recently occurred, and had happened very fast, taking the world a bit by surprise," says Hajdu. "That meant that people had just dropped everything at work and left to go to their families. Then they either barricaded themselves in, left town, became zombies, or died. That meant abandoned cars—some wrecks, but a lot that were just left behind—which we dusted to show time had passed. We had to show panicked flight, then neglect

ABOVE: Trash blankets, easily set up and removed by the set dressers, litter the streets and alleys of Atlanta.

OPPOSITE: The rooftops of downtown Atlanta initially provided a safe refuge for the survivors, but danger soon flooded the buildings.

and abandonment, mostly by the judicious use of debris."

This was a case where working on a TV show schedule meant that the design team had to come up with time-saving solutions, especially since they were often called on to dress larger-scale locations like city streets. A little ingenuity led Hajdu to create what he refers to as "trash blankets." "In order to quickly and efficiently dress a street or row of houses with trash or mounds of dead vegetation, the set dressers glued newspaper, plastic bottles, cans, clothing,

et cetera, to weed-barrier cloth," he explains. "They made large, lightweight 'trash assemblages' that hung together and could be thrown into the gutters, under cars, in the middle of streets, on lawns, et cetera—and not blow away. They would be harmless to the locations, quickly struck, and reusable." The production team did the same with dead leaves and artificial vines and weeds to create "leaf blankets" for scenes outside the city. The blankets were roughly three by eight feet and various other sizes, and required only two people to trash a location on the morning of the shoot.

Beyond dressing the areas with the trash and leaf blankets, Hajdu credits the work of Set Decorator Lisa Alkofer for creating the postapocalyptic look they needed. "[She] did an amazing job finding unique set dressing that looked like people had taken belongings as they tried to escape the zombie apocalypse, and had abandoned them like the settlers crossing the prairie."

Since they could not distress or paint people's houses, they needed to find areas that looked abandoned and neglected from the start. "With the help of Michael J. Riley, our location manager," says Hajdu, "and judicious scouting in both urban and residential sections of Atlanta, we were able to find the look we needed." This work further established the look of the television version of *The Walking Dead*, and allowed the series to be primarily filmed on locations in and around Atlanta.

SIX

LAND OF THE DEAD

During the pilot, Rick Grimes makes his journey from his home to what he believes will be his salvation in Atlanta. Over the next few episodes, the characters spend time in and around the zombie-plagued city, while Rick and Shane debate whether they should stay or leave. The answer could, and does, mean life or death to the survivors. Although those discussions are central to the first season of the series on-screen, no such conversations happened among the production staff. They knew they'd found the perfect setting for their series from the start.

"Atlanta is very much a character in Robert's comic book," says Executive Producer Gale Anne Hurd. "There were panels that were almost duplicated, in terms of the visuals. It did root us, and it rooted the cast in a world that is proto-typical America. It was urban, and yet with nature all around."

The natural elements of the location were a benefit to the production, both in terms of the look of the series and the metaphor behind it. "Here in Los Angeles, everything turns brown," Hurd continues. "Whereas in Atlanta in the summer, everything is lush and green. It's almost a tremendous juxtaposition to the decay of the zombies and the dread that our characters live with, which I think is really interesting."

The producers were able to work with the city and state governments to get access to downtown Atlanta so they could bring a realistic portrayal of destruction and desola-tion to a major city. "We're very lucky work-ing in Atlanta," says the pilot episode's direc-tor of photography, David Tattersall. "It's an extremely film-friendly city, and the produc-tion was able to take over a large area of the downtown center. Several city blocks were blocked off, and we were able to create that sort of postapocalyptic violence."

The abandoned streets of Atlanta overrun by the undead were key to developing a con-vincing postapocalyptic world for the audience. Without those scenes of devastation, the series would have been a much smaller-scale produc-tion that could have had a more difficult time capturing the imagination of the audience. But simply securing the streets was not enough. The production design team needed to do a lot of work to transform several blocks of a vibrant and functioning city into a zombie war zone.

"Dressing downtown Atlanta was our largest logistical and scheduling challenge," says Production Designer Greg Melton. "The con-cept was that a section of Atlanta had become a green zone where the military could protect a certain square-block area. Basically, the thought is that Rick approaches this military checkpoint that's been overrun. We had lots of abandoned cars with luggage or doors open, like some people had tried to run the blockade."

ABOVE: At times, Rick's silent ride into Atlanta almost perfectly matched the "storyboard" created by the comic book pages.

PREVIOUS SPREAD: After closing several streets of downtown Atlanta, the production team worked to give the city a ghost-town atmosphere. Sometimes this re-quired digitally removing vehicles and ambient noise.

ABOVE: A preliminary design concept for the abandoned checkpoint that served as the setting for the climactic Walker attack at the end of the pilot and for Rick's escape at the opening of episode 2.

The production design team dressed more than twenty-five vehicles, including a Huey helicopter and a sixty-ton tank over a six-block area. "All of this had to be done starting at 7 P.M. Friday night to be ready at 6 A.M. Saturday for the company to shoot," Melton explains. "It was a tricky set that had to be carefully designed to accommodate the heavy equipment needed to place the vehicles, many of which did not run."

Alex Hajdu, who was still in the role of art director in the early episodes, notes that the prep work that went into the preproduction of the scene was key to achieving their goal. As with the earlier gas station shoot, using Google

Earth aided in planning the placement of the derelict vehicles. "We knew all of the angles, so we knew exactly what to prepare," he says. "The exteriors of the local stores either gave permission to use their names or we blanked them out. The courthouse was not to be touched at all in any way." They had to shoot on a weekend, when the downtown area is less congested, and get everything in and out on a tight schedule.

Since the characters would return in later episodes, the production wound up shooting twice at that location. The second time, they had to match the debris to the first to avoid any continuity problems. It was quite an impressive

"RIDE INTO ATLANTA" STORYBOARDS

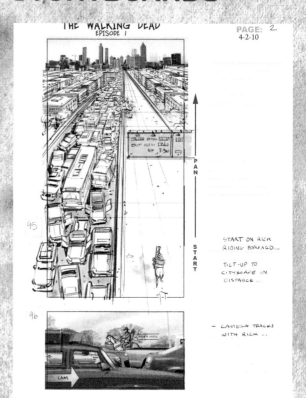

99/4

·PAN.1

LONG LENS SHOT —
A STREET FULL OF
WALKERS. START WALKERS
TURNED AWAY FROM US...
- ALL THE WALKER TURN
FORWARD IN UNISON...

99/5

- ON RICK - REACTS
IN HORROR...

99/6

PAN 1

IN

IN

RICK TURNS HIS
HORSE AROUND AS
THE MOB OF
WALKERS SURGES
FORWARD

CONTINUE

ABOVE: Numerous vehicles, including this burned-out bus, were dressed to appear hastily abandoned during a tumultuous battle.

feat, as the large vehicles were not the only elements that had to be re-created on the streets. "We also fabricated fake concrete K-rails, such as you would see on the freeways, to use as barricades and gun emplacements," Hajdu explains. "This added a sense of a 'last stand at the courthouse' military checkpoint. We wanted to show that nothing could stop the onslaught of the zombie hordes—even tanks, machine guns, troops. The set decorators made sandbags filled with sawdust on wheeled carriages so barricades could be pre-built and moved to camera." Many of the vehicles and other military elements were reused in episodes 5 and 6 for the scenes shot outside the CDC.

Oftentimes, productions can take shortcuts by only dressing part of a scene and keeping the cameras in tight, but this was not the case on *The Walking Dead*. Frank Darabont really wanted to showcase the devastation in whatever ways he could. "We always shot with multiple cameras," says Hajdu. "So we often needed to dress to multiple angles." This meant that they would need more than just bits of debris and trash to

fill the area. "The transportation department did a fantastic job," he continues. "They found an incredible burned-out bus, which was better than anything we could have created, and many wrecked cars, including a burned-out police car."

Another highlighted vehicle on that set was the tank sitting abandoned on the street. This was another element from the comic book which found itself with an expanded role in the television series. In the comic, Rick and Glenn pass by the tank when they make their return trip into the city for guns. Here, it becomes an important set piece for the cliff-hanger ending of the pilot.

"The M1 Abrams tank came from a local collector, Doug Cole," explains Hajdu. "He also provided tank parts and technical advisors to us for the tank interior mock-up, as well as a Huey for the exterior of the hospital where Rick emerges from his coma and enters into his new

ABOVE: The M1 Abrams tank, on loan from a local collector, was the centerpiece of the action at the climax of the pilot.

OPPOSITE: The tank was a callback to one Rick and Glenn pass on their zombie-gut-coated stroll deeper into Atlanta in issue no. 4.

ABOVE: The tank interior was designed to match the actual vehicle while allowing for the requirements of filming on a soundstage. It was one of the few constructed sets used during the pilot.

nightmare reality. . . . Doug actually owns two M1 tanks, and he used the one with the street-legal treads that don't tear up the asphalt for this scene."

To shoot Rick as he crawled under the tank in a last-ditch effort to escape, Darabont took inspiration from a rig he and Melton had invented when they were teens shooting their own movies on Super 8. They asked Key Grip Richard Mark to create a dolly system with a long aluminum frame on rollers to track under the tank. "We made a fairly crude sort of tilt pan head that was controlled with ropes," explains Tattersall. "It had a twenty-four-foot reach, so it was able to track the full length to the tank as Rick was crawling underneath."

The interior of the tank was one of the only sets built for the pilot, since everything else was filmed on location to heighten the realism. They built a hatch matching the tank that Rick enters on location and, once he's inside, they went to the stage. "The tank set was designed to come apart to allow filming inside it," explains Melton. "We dressed the interior with actual tank equipment, supplied to us by Doug Cole,

and we made the interior about a foot wider to help get the dynamic shots inside."

To meet the full needs of the production, simply dressing the downtown area with practical set pieces was not enough. More than just tanks and buses filled this space. When Rick turns the corner in the pilot and comes face-to-undead-face with a horde of zombies, the true action begins.

The technical requirements for shooting the zombie-filled streets as the undead swarm Rick called for the visual effects team to re-create those streets digitally so that they could manipulate the scenes. "We built four city blocks in complete 3-D," says Visual Effects Supervisor Sam Nicholson. "Almost like a photoreal video game, if you will. It was matched exactly to the buildings." To do this, production took a photo survey of the site and provided images of every one of the existing buildings to the 3-D group so they could build entirely duplicate city blocks. Once that was done, they matched the two realities together, blending the physical world and the virtual world exactly, because they had an exact model of both.

From there, they needed to add an almost unheard-of number of zombies to create the climatic final image of the pilot. Dozens of zombie extras swarm the tank in which Rick has found refuge, while hundreds upon hundreds more are drawn to the area. To hire, train, and make-up all those extras would have been too great a task to do on a TV show schedule and budget, so they needed to be created digitally.

"With the 3-D zombies that we were adding, that just brings an extra layer of complexity to the overall compositing because the motion of how zombies move and how they walk all has to be refined," says Visual Effects Supervisor Jason Sperling. "We actually did a motion capture session with a handpicked extra who had gone to zombie school. We were able to capture his motion, and then duplicate that over hundreds, if not thousands of zombie extras. That allowed their motion to feel like the motion of the practical zombies that were actually on set."

Working on the streets of Atlanta allowed the production crew to re-create another memorable moment from the comic book in episode 2: Rick and Glenn, covered in zombie remains to hide their scent, moving, unnoticed, through a horde of Walkers. To properly play that scene required the production crew to manipulate the weather as a change from sunny skies to a sudden burst of rain.

"It's one thing to piece together a scene with this kind of requirement on a feature film,

ABOVE: Rick flees the zombie horde in the final scene of the pilot. Composed of over a hundred extras, the horde grew with the help of additional computer-generated Walkers.

"That scene was awesome. It was kind of my 'Welcome to Showbiz' moment. All the other things we had done up to then was kind of 'normal,' I guess. If you can call it that. Basically, we had been shooting a lot of footage without the aid of visual effects (for us). But that day when I walked on to set and they had a trench coat for me and then just started covering us in crap, I said, 'Whoa. This is kind of legit.' But I think it didn't fully hit me until we started tearing down a main street in downtown Atlanta, with one hundred zombie background actors chasing us while three rain machines poured rain down, all while a cart was speeding down along side us filming it. I loved filming that scene, I could have done it all day."

—Steven Yeun

ABOVE: All aspects of the production came together to create the complex sequence during which Rick and Glenn flee as the rain washes away their zombie-gut camouflage and Walkers pick up their human scent.

OPPOSITE: Two episodes of the television series were a reinterpretation of the pages of issue no. 4 in which Rick and Glenn go back into the city to obtain more guns.

where production time is a little less of a consideration," says the episode's D.P., David Boyd. "With our schedule, I used every subterfuge I ever learned to keep the day aimed at telling the story of the weather. Even when the weather is such a central part of a scene, as it was in this scene, it's still one of the biggest challenges in my line of work to see through to its rightful conclusion on a TV schedule. There are so many competing pressures on a production day."

Complicating things even more was the fact that the weather that particular day was bright sunlight going in and out of clouds. "I had to commit to a setup without any assurance the real weather would be appropriate to it," Boyd continues. "Only by guile and bluster did I manage to get the weather correct that day, and whatever I couldn't, I either softened the sun overhead to make things overcast, or blew big lights onto the scene to make a cloudy day look like it was sunny."

To create the rain, the production looked to Special Effects Coordinator Darrell Pritchett, who used overhead sprinkler rigs to drench the Atlanta streets and the actors. "We put a lot of water out there," he says. "Some of the shot was dictated by what we could accomplish. Obviously, the director looks in a direction and says, 'I want rain, and I want it there.' I do think [visual effects] extended the rain just a little bit on the far end, but the rest of it was pretty much practical."

Once Rick and Glenn get through the rain, they're able to grab a truck and make their escape, but it would not be their last foray into the city. The characters, and the production, would be back on another weekend not only to re-create the street where Rick left his gun bag, but to explore new sets as well. In "Vatos," the key set inside the city limits was a gang hangout that was secretly a front for a nursing home. "I thought the script did a great job of using the

EPISODE 5: "WILDFIRE"

Written by Glen Mazzara
Directed by Ernest Dickerson

RICK:...Atlanta isn't what we thought. It's not what they promised. The city is...Do not enter the city. It belongs to the dead now.

SYNOPSIS: The morning after the Walker attack, Rick tries to warn Morgan away from Atlanta, but there's no way to be sure his message gets through over the walkie-talkie.

In camp, Andrea sits vigil over Amy's body while the others burn the Walker remains and bury their friends. But first they have to make sure that the dead don't return. Carol chooses to be the one to take an ax to her husband's head, drawing strength from her conflicted emotions over his death.

Jacqui notices Jim bleeding as they clean up the camp. He tries to play it off, but he can't hide the truth: He's been bitten. It's only a matter of time before he turns. The group debates what to do about him. Rick suggests they go to the CDC for help, but Shane doesn't agree and no one can come to a consensus on the situation.

Numerous people in the group try to reason with Andrea, but she won't let them take her sister's body from her. When Dale comes to pay his respects, Andrea gives her sister the necklace she picked up in the city as a birthday gift. Amy slowly reawakens, giving Andrea the chance to apologize for the times she wasn't around. But Andrea is there for her sister now, and she shoots Amy in the head to end her suffering.

Lori eventually sides with Rick about going to the CDC, much to Shane's disappointment. They still leave the discussion without a resolution as the two men go off to sweep the woods for more Walkers. When Shane has Rick in his gun sights, he pauses to consider pulling the trigger, but stops himself before he makes an irreversible decision. Dale is a witness to the moment, but Shane acts like it was all just an accident.

Upon their return to camp, Shane announces that he's thought about Rick's plan and now agrees that they should leave for the CDC in the morning. The Morales family decides to split off from the group and search for their relatives in Birmingham.

CONTINUED

Rick and Shane give them some guns and ammunition as everyone says farewell to their friends.

Jim's condition is getting worse as the now-smaller group hits the road. He won't make it all the way to the CDC. Dale suggests what he tried to say earlier: that they should let Jim choose his own fate. Jim decides to be left on the side of the road outside the city so he can turn and maybe be reunited with the family he left behind.

Elsewhere outside of Atlanta, a lone CDC scientist named Jenner files a report: It is Day 194 since Wildfire was declared and sixty-three days since the disease abruptly went global. A full decontamination of his lab destroyed the last of his tissue samples, prompting him to file what will likely be his last report. Tomorrow he plans to blow his brains out.

The group of survivors arriving outside the building may change that. Rick and the others are pounding on an exterior door, begging to get in as they are almost overwhelmed by Walkers. Rick's family and friends are screaming for him to run with them, but he won't listen. He believes that their only salvation lies inside the building. His pleas for help are answered when the door finally opens.

ABOVE: The gang hangout in episode 4 had no counterpart in the comic series, giving the production team the freedom to surprise the readers with something new.

audience's preconception of who the 'Vatos' (the gang members) were, and then surprising us with who they 'become' later," says Hajdu.

The production design team needed to come up with a set that would contribute to that first impression by adding to the menace of the supposed gang. "The location of their hideout was a fantastic brick factory/warehouse complex," says Hajdu. "Parts of it were converted into a series of artists' studios, and the rest was either a crumbling ruin or had working machine shops inside. The exterior I chose was an area that was created when a factory building roof burned and caved in, exposing the interior. This created a macabre courtyard of rubble and partially collapsed walls. There were openings leading to nowhere and gaping windows that made it feel threatening. Rick and the guys have to cross this no-man's-land to get to the warehouse entrance. It was like a Sergio Leone spaghetti western, like *Once Upon a Time in the West.* You expected to see the silhouettes of bandits on the roof. The courtyard became like the street of an old western town where the showdown takes place."

Darabont wanted the gang to make dramatic entrances and exits, so Hajdu designed a pair of distressed sliding wooden factory doors that fit an existing opening in the courtyard. The interior set was in another building entirely that met their needs for the hangout. "It was wonderfully layered with old equipment and large windows partially obscured by racks, pallets, and other dark shapes," says Hajdu.

The place was almost too perfect, and they had to remove some elements to make room for cars to give the appearance that the gang was stripping vehicles for parts and stockpiling supplies. "It was a cool take on the urban survivalist stereotype," Hajdu notes. "These were streetwise tough guys, and this was their hangout. It also underscored the implied stereotype of the gangbanger, which was important for the later reveal."

Set Decorator Lisa Alkofer created areas for the gang members within that space to give it a more lived-in feel, including a bar and a barbecue/kitchen area. "It was a clubhouse and a gang headquarters and a working garage all in one," says Hajdu. "It allowed Rick and the others to walk into the heart of the gang's space and be instantly surrounded by them for the big showdown. It also was the place where, at the height of tension—with everyone pointing loaded guns at each other, the complete stand-off—the grandmother wanders in, breaking the bubble."

At that point, the audience discovers that these tough guys are actually the caregivers and protectors of the elderly residents of an adjacent nursing home. The two distinctly different sets presented Hajdu with the challenge of creating a believable transition from warehouse to nursing home, with the latter actually located across town and having a very different architectural style. "The nursing home location was a working church," he explains. "It was a concrete building, but had a rear section that was partially brick. Next door was a low building also of brick. I designed eight-foot-high concrete block walls that tied architecturally with the church exterior."

They added neglected vegetation and sad patio furniture, and covered the asphalt with dead leaves and mulch so the actors could enter from the alley between the church and a chain-link fence and cross this outdoor area into the nursing home. "I did a 3-D SketchUp model to illustrate the results," Hajdu says. "The fact that the walls were so high and solid helped sell the idea the zombies wouldn't see the elderly folks or the Vatos coming and going from the hideout and the home."

The city streets of Atlanta provided the production crew with much of what they needed for the first season of *The Walking Dead*, but nothing compared to the treasure trove they found on the outskirts of town. The campsite where Shane and Lori and the other survivors take refuge was an important part of the first six issues of the comic book, and the production was lucky to find exactly what they needed only about five miles from downtown Atlanta. Hurd explains, "When our location manager, Mike Riley, and line producer, Tom Luse, took us there, we were pinching ourselves. We could not

ABOVE: The quarry with the Atlanta skyline in the background provided everything the production needed from the location without requiring computer-generated enhancements.

THAT'S *DALE* UP THERE KEEPING WATCH. THAT'S HIS CAMPER. *JIM* IS OVER THERE EATING.

THAT'S *CAROL* AND HER DAUGHTER *SOPHIA* SITTING ON THE BACK OF THE CAR.

believe there was a location so close to downtown Atlanta that actually—as scripted—had the skyline of Atlanta in the shot. It did not have to be added digitally. And that if you were a group of survivors you would choose that location with ready water and where you were far enough from town that you were relatively safe from a zombie attack—although as we come to find out, not that safe—and yet close enough that Glenn can make his forays into town for supplies. And it was stunningly beautiful."

The producers weren't the only ones excited about the location. Melton is quick to note, "We fell in love with its skyscraper view of downtown and the dramatic cliffs above the quarry. We took what nature gave us there and created the realistic campsite with campfires and laundry lines. We nestled all the tents in the tree line and gave the RV the high ground for Dale to watch over them."

Almost every member of the production team enjoyed working in that space, but none more so than Director of Photography David Boyd. "I so looked forward to photographing it," he says. "Darabont chose to locate the camp on a cliff overlooking a deep, water-filled quarry, our characters requiring water to survive. The idea that there are different physical levels at play, which convey concepts of emotional tone when photographed correctly, goes back to John Ford's *The Searchers* and before. It remains a marvelous way for an audience to begin to feel the emotions of all that goes on. I love the pastoral setting down within the quarry, but only when viewed against the rough life in the camp above. Darabont set up a similar structure in the second episode,

where anything at street level in Atlanta was very dangerous, and things were a little safer up on rooftops and down in tunnels underground. It was fitting that most of the beautiful stone that built the great buildings of Atlanta was quarried out of the lake, and you can see those buildings from the camp atop the quarry."

In laying out the campsite at the quarry, the design team kept in mind that, as established in the comic, it would eventually come under siege by zombies. From the first episode, the campsite was designed to allow for the attack without having to rework the camp's layout.

ABOVE: The camp scenes were filmed largely on location, though some work was done on a soundstage.

OPPOSITE: Dale's RV (as seen in this panel from issue no. 3) is a major set piece in the comic book series as it is the primary mode of transportation for the survivors.

At times, greenery was added to block certain views, but otherwise, it was simply a matter of creating a basic campsite. "For the most part, the camp came together very organically and used the space well, with enough random elements to make it feel real," says Hajdu. "Each character had their tent and belongings that reflected that character's backstory."

AMY'S RESURRECTION

ABOVE: Emma Bell was dressed in a temporary tattoo of blood to allow for a more comfortable filming experience than the traditional Karo syrup–based mixture would provide.

In the comic book, Andrea makes the unimaginable decision to shoot her sister mere minutes after the zombie attack. As with many other moments in the television series, the writers chose to linger on that event and give it the proper room to breathe. At the opening of episode 5, "Wildfire," Andrea has already kept vigil over her sister's body throughout the night and into the next day. She refuses to listen as her friends try to convince her to let go, even pulling a gun on Rick at one point. When the time finally comes for Amy to reawaken, Andrea is there for her sister. She says good-bye and pulls the trigger, shooting Amy in the head. It is a highly charged scene for the actresses, who got a bit of an assist from the resident zombie expert.

Greg Nicotero explains how he contributed more than just makeup effects to the scene: "A lot of the actors, they didn't grow up watching the same movies that Frank and I watched. I could quote horror movies from the '70s and '80s. But a lot of the actors didn't have the fanatical obsession like Frank and I do. It's something that he and I share, of course. . . . I spent a lot of time with Laurie Holden, because she really wanted to understand the emotional impact of how that character would react. How many times has she seen this before? If she really believes that by staring at Amy and holding her that maybe she can get through. All that kind of stuff. It wasn't just a makeup effects gig for me. I actually had an opportunity to help the actors understand the genre."

The strategic use of blood in that scene served as an ever-present reminder of the violence of the world that preceded the equally violent action Andrea was about to take.

The last thing either of the actresses needed was to be distracted by special effects makeup on their bodies in the emotionally charged scene. "The formula we use for fake blood has got corn syrup in it," Nicotero explains. "So after fifteen minutes it gets sticky, and it's really horribly uncomfortable, especially with Amy's death. Not only were we pumping blood out of her arm and pumping blood out of her neck, but then she has to lay on the ground for the rest of that day of shooting and the next day of shooting."

When they were shooting the night of the attack, they first pumped the traditional corn syrup–based blood out of her arm for the actual bites. After a few takes when they knew they'd gotten their shot, they cleaned her off and switched over to a solution made of alcohol-soluble pigments to simulate the blood, which they could paint on like a temporary tattoo. They used the same solution when they filmed the scene where Andrea cradles Amy in her arms. "It still was really sticky," Nicotero admits. "Laurie was cradling [Emma] and smearing the blood around so they were sticky, even though we tried to do the best we could to accommodate for that."

ABOVE: A close-up of the second wound inflicted on Emma Bell by Greg Nicotero's zombie.

Either way, the scene achieved the effect Darabont was hoping for when the writing team decided to include it in their story. "Emma Bell getting killed is a total mindfuck at the end of episode 4," Darabont proclaims. "It's like, 'Oh my God, it's so shocking and horrible and just disturbing.' She was one that I really regretted killing, although she was always going to die. That character died in Kirkman's comic books, so I always knew, hiring Emma Bell, that she was gonna get lunched. . . . But when it came time to do it . . . she's so sweet—she's such a lovely girl, and she played sisters with Laurie Holden so well. I mean, these were like two peas in a pod, and I loved their characters together. So when it came time to ruthlessly have her killed by zombies, it was a regret. I'm going to miss this character. I'm going to miss this person. She is so sweet, and she's been so interesting, and their dynamic as sisters has been so rewarding—I'm really going to miss her. But then you have to follow through on your original intention."

Even though the campsite was perfect for the daylight scene—where it could show the Atlanta skyline or highlight the quarry in its best light—for nighttime shots, the crew discussed bringing everything inside to a soundstage. A soundstage version of the set was created, but was used minimally as the preference was to film as much as possible outdoors. Boyd felt very strongly about the natural filming location. "I'll usually always advocate for shooting in a real place," he says. "There was some pressure to shoot the campfire scenes on a warehouse soundstage. I voted for the real location because there's wind and bugs about, smoke and actor[s'] hair moves correctly, and we could see all the rest of the campsite rather than cheat the life out of it all."

Once they got the go-ahead to shoot the real location for the night scenes, they set about designing and fabricating small lights that could stand up to the heat of a real campfire. "Firelight rarely has enough strength to get a great image on film," Boyd notes. "We chased our little fire lights up and down to make the effect believable and warmed them up with straw-colored gel. The story required us to keep the flames low and build high fire rings so that any zombies happening by wouldn't be drawn to the encampment. So we denied ourselves a high flame and relied on the slow glow of a low flame and embers. In close-up, especially, this effect works quite nicely. Because the actors were actually outside in a real place, one they were all very familiar with, I think this helped them believe in their work also."

Off camera, the production crew used real flame to light elements in which sound wasn't a big consideration, since propane flames make a high-pitched noise. Beyond that, they strategically allowed the forest around the camp to fall off into black to emphasize its isolation. "Oftentimes, we'd put three cameras on a campfire scene at the same time so we'd be able to cut scenes together that match movements perfectly, and performances have a real-time connection with each other," Boyd notes. "It's really a beautiful way to work."

For the daytime scenes, the propane flames served a more practical purpose in the shots where the survivors burned the bodies of the Walkers who had invaded their camp. "We really weren't burning anything other than propane," Special Effects Coordinator Darrell Pritchett notes. "Add in some smoke and what have you to enhance it. The bodies themselves—if you look at it, you'll see that nothing's being consumed."

In spite of the beauty of filming on location by night or day, there are definite drawbacks involved. Not only does the weather have to cooperate, but the world around the location has to as well. This is especially important when trying to re-create a postapocalyptic world in which an eerie silence pervades every moment of the day. "You're recording sound in very difficult circumstances at times," explains Darabont. "Some of our locations were—*oh my God*—the noise. For the noise on the rooftop, for example, we had to cleverly lay in sounds of wind on top to eliminate sounds of distant traffic. Or with people at camp talking around the campfire, the crickets must've been in season. There's more bug noises than you can imagine.

When you're watching the show, we didn't lay those crickets in—those crickets were there."

Still, it's something that Darabont doesn't mind dealing with when it enhances the scene. "To me it's all part of the texture of reality that lands on the soundtrack and gets worked into the movie," he says. "Sometimes the noise is just unacceptable, because we also had trains and stuff. Then you have to do a little dialogue replacement in postproduction. But I tried to keep as much of the original dialogue tracks as possible, because that's where the best performance usually is."

The production also had to deal with sunlight. With his years of experience, David Tattersall is well-versed in the proper way to use the natural light to its maximum benefit. "The best way I found to approach the exterior work is to try and shoot the location clockwise," he says. "So you try to arrange it so that you start the day shooting into the east, and then slowly wind your way around the clock throughout the day so that you try and keep the backlight. Hopefully, you're playing south by the middle of the day, and hopefully you're playing west by the end of the day. So, that's a good first plan. And save the wide shots for the better-looking parts of the day when the light is low and cross-lighting your location."

With the sun comes the heat, which was a particular problem during the filming of the first season. Atlanta experienced one of the hottest summers on record in 2010, just when the production was ramping up. "It just took a tremendous amount out of you every day," says Darabont. "I had to wear towels soaked in ice water on my head—on my baldpate—to keep from passing out a few times, it was so hot. And the humidity was staggering. You'd sweat through your clothes all day long, and yet people still brought their A game. They brought their best to the set."

Boyd echoes that enthusiasm. "Nothing slowed us down; not the elements, not anything. We had wind and rain, thunder and lightning, heat and humidity beyond belief, and we always found something productive to shoot. I recall running for cover from lightning one afternoon into Glenn's car up on blocks. While it's true a TV schedule is daunting, I like to approach that, and similar constraints, as good things. . . . The rigors of production we endured to make these episodes can't be believed, but what we got was, I think, an accurate line on the graphic novel and a very real feel to the story of these characters on the brink of extinction."

Even a born-and-bred Atlanta native like young Chandler Riggs found the temperature unusually warm that summer. "We stayed cool by going into the RV; they put an air-conditioning thing in there," Riggs says. "Crew members were putting umbrellas over us and the makeup people were giving us these freezing washcloths."

By the time the production moved on to episode 6 at the CDC, everyone was more than ready to film indoors. Of course, that had its own issues, according to Riggs: "The problem was, that it started getting too cold inside. We started to have to bring jackets!"

SEVEN

POSTMORTEM:

EXAMINATIONS ON POSTPRODUCTION

Once the production wraps filming on an episode, the work is still far from done, especially on a series like *The Walking Dead*. Postproduction is an integral part of any television show. It's when the editors cut together the scenes, the composer and music supervisor add the music, and the visual effects team works their computer-generated magic. *The Walking Dead* may not seem like a typical genre show since there are no superspecial science-fiction effects. Aside from Dr. Jenner's digital presentation in episode 6, there aren't even computer simulations of dead bodies like in a forensics series. In fact, the visual effects on this television series work best when you don't notice them at all.

OPPOSITE: Not all graduates of zombie school needed to worry about the proper shuffling walk, as some were prop bodies used as set decoration.

In the comic book industry, there is often a focus on how the "special effects" on any given page have the potential to be far superior to the visuals that could be created with an equivalent TV show budget. But Tony Moore and Charlie Adlard's artwork in *The Walking Dead* isn't about the flash-bang super-hero whooshes of color and sparkling powers. It is intentionally stark and realistic. To approximate that for the television screen required a different approach both in filming and in manipulating that film when shooting wrapped.

One of the things Robert Kirkman appreciates most about the television version of his comic series is how it achieves the scale of the postapocalyptic world. In the comic books, they don't have to close streets or make sure there aren't any cars driving by to create the illusion of a lifeless setting. Thanks to the postproduction assist from the visual effects team, neither does the television series. As Kirkman points out, "There's a ton of computer-generated effects in the show that you would never know were there."

From the added debris outside the hospital to the cars you don't see on the highway as Rick rides into Atlanta, Visual Effects Supervisor Sam Nicholson gives a great deal of credit to the advancements in digital effects over the past decade. "That's why they're invisible," he says. "And that was the mandate, by the way: that you should never, ever look at any shot in *The Walking Dead* and feel that you're looking at something that's been manipulated."

Admittedly, calling it postproduction is a bit of a misnomer, as the visual effects work starts as early in the preproduction stage as possible. Producing film-quality work on a television budget and schedule presents a familiar challenge to the team, as the effects house has also worked on series like *Heroes* and *24*. "You establish a pattern budget at the beginning of the season and say, 'We're going to do ten of these, and they should cost *x*.' And hopefully, they will."

When the scripts come in, that's when they see what the writers have developed from the initial conversations at the start of the season. Oftentimes, the visuals are two or three times larger than they were when in preproduction. "The great thing about Frank is that as a writer/director, he understands how he can change the creative [capital] to help make all the departments work," says Nicholson. "He knows where he has to have his punch. But if you say, 'Look, this is really going to be expensive, and we're not going to get to that bang. Do you really want to spend the money here or would you rather spend it downstream a little bit where you need the pop?' Being a writer/director, he can make those kinds of changes, and it makes for a very fluid creative process."

That process involves more than just Darabont. To enhance the visuals in any scene, the effects team has to work with the other departments jointly so that everyone is on the same page. "It's necessarily an enjoyable give-and-take," says David Boyd. "We listen to each other. On the one hand, I must deliver what the visual effects team needs in order to do what we've all talked about. On the other, I have the clearest view of all the scenes we've ever done, because I've been physically present at all of them and I had a lot to do with how they were set up. I know how visual effects can help tell the story. I know what makes the most sense to spend visual effects money on. The VFX team on *The Walking Dead* has done a masterful job integrating their work into the design and photography, really making believable some pivotal sequences."

Over the course of the series, the visual effects team had a hand in every single episode. This work was intentionally designed to go largely unnoticed. The viewers should not have realized that the exterior walls of the "Vatos" hangout had nothing behind them or that sometimes, cars drove through the backgrounds of some scenes. But the most pivotal sequence on which the visual effects team worked is one that didn't fade into the scenery. In fact, it was the biggest moment in the course of the series from a visual standpoint: the destruction of the Centers for Disease Control and Prevention in the season finale.

The group's decision to visit the CDC and its subsequent destruction were a story line entirely unique to the television series. Kirkman freely admits he hadn't even realized that the CDC was in Atlanta when he wrote the early issues of the comic. To Darabont, having the headquarters of the one place in the world the survivors might go to for answers existing literally on the other side of town was too big a coincidence to ignore. "Those are the kind of detours I'm talking about as we follow Robert's storytelling toward the distant horizon," Darabont explains. "Let's jump off the path and go rummage

around in this dark corner of our brains and see what fun or horrible storytelling we can add to the mythos of *The Walking Dead*."

In designing the explosion of the CDC, the actual work began with the location manager and the production design team. For the visual effects department to know how to create the explosion they would eventually have to produce, they needed to know, first and foremost, what the building would look like.

When Production Designer Alex Hajdu began to conceive the interior design for the CDC building, he had yet to receive the complete script for episode 5 and only had an outline for episode 6. This is not unusual on a television schedule, but it did force him to develop ideas for the space without knowing what would happen in it. Thankfully, Darabont was very flexible in making adjustments to the scripts after he visited the locations for the interior and exterior shots and saw what they had to work with. Hajdu credits this collaboration with Darabont and the directors on the two final episodes of the season for creating a synergy that contributed to the success of the setting.

ABOVE: The ramp leading to the command center platform was added so Jenner could wheel a piano into the space for a scene that was cut prior to filming.

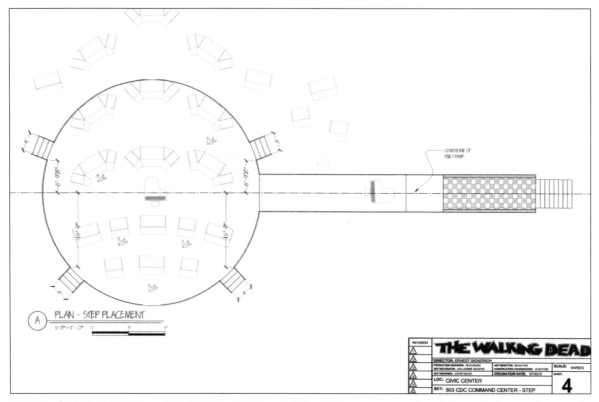

A   PLAN - STEP PLACEMENT
1/8" = 1' - 0"

ABOVE: One of several blueprints detailing the layout of the CDC command center platform that were drawn up to show the set from multiple angles and elevations.

"When I read the script, it felt very Cold War to me, in a Kubrick kind of way," Hajdu explains. "Of course the image of the war room in *Dr. Strangelove* came to mind. I felt nothing better illustrated the futility of a powerful government institution faced with an unsolvable dilemma than that symbolic film reference. To further underscore that futility, I knew I needed a set with some scale. I also knew that I could not afford to build a giant set like *WarGames* on a television budget. I needed to take it in a slightly more theatrical direction, using the space itself instead of building walls. Sometimes, limitations help define style."

The locations they chose for the interior scenes were inside the Atlanta Convention Center. "It was vast and had a modern, hard-edge look to the interior," says Hajdu. "The walls were painted charcoal and steel gray. The ceiling was black and had air ducts and lighting grids—fantastic texture we could 'feel' if there was any light spill from the set. It even had upstairs offices and hallways that fit the story line for the survivors to take up residence in the seemingly safe environment."

With thoughts of *Dr. Strangelove* swimming through his head, Hajdu started searching for a large circular lighting truss to be the centerpiece of the main set, finding one that was thirty feet in diameter. "I needed to separate the control room area from the rest of the space," he continues. "So we built a four-by-sixty-foot round platform with railings and stairs, and gave it a satin black surface, with the circular lighting truss overhead. It seemed to float in the space. I had to cover the concrete floor to complete the feeling of isolation and separation."

His next challenge was to fill the platform with control consoles. After a quote for shipping the necessary units from Los Angeles proved to be cost-prohibitive, Hajdu went back to a prior location they had scouted. The former site of the Atlanta 911 Emergency Center had exactly the equipment he wanted. "There were rooms filled with communications center console racks that had their electronics stripped out," he says. "We were able to make a rental deal to acquire them. All we had to do was dummy some smoked Plexi monitor screens with bezels and add task lighting and seating." The giant video screen on which Jenner makes his presentation was added by the visual effects team in postproduction. The design team simply provided the truss legs that held up the nonexistent screen.

For the exterior of the CDC, the production team chose the Cobb Energy Performing Arts Centre, which they would also use to film the interior lobby and the room where the generator was located. "The interior lobby had a giant built-in mural that we had to hide," says Hajdu. "I designed a large CDC logo floating over a satellite image of Earth to cover it, which looked interesting reflected in the glass doors on the inside."

When Hajdu received the final scripts for episodes 5 and 6, he knew he had to work with that huge glass curtain wall and the glass doors in the lobby, which presented him with an interesting challenge. "Our characters had

to find this building in a state of emergency lockdown, surrounded by tanks, artillery, and dead soldiers; a heavily fortified and defended CDC that's had its exterior overrun by zombies, but secured from entry," he says. "They too were locked out of the building, on the ragged edge, with the zombies starting to converge on them. But there also had to be a way to admit them when they finally made contact with Edwin Jenner."

Hajdu used security shutters that would have come down in an emergency to seal the building. "We built facades using metal garage door shutters, painting everything with a satin aluminum finish to match the Cobb exterior," he says. "I designed some CDC emergency graphics on the doors that would only be revealed when the doors came crashing down."

His work was instrumental in the powerful ending to "Wildfire," in which one of the security doors opens for Rick and the others, showing them the light at the end of their proverbial tunnel and potential salvation inside. But those doors also presented a problem for the route the survivors would take in their later escape. "The last challenge was to get the characters out of the building, which was still in a state of lockdown with security shutters in place. When Frank came to the location survey, I commented on all the glass that was still exposed, that wasn't behind a shutter. There was too much of it, in my opinion. What was to stop these crazed and desperate people—who only had minutes to spare before the building exploded—from breaking the glass and getting out?"

Darabont's answer came in the next draft of the script, designating the glass to be bulletproof and virtually indestructible. The characters must use the grenade Rick took with him when he escaped the tank in episode 2, resulting in the first of two explosions in the season-ending episode. To allow for their escape, the production team had a professional glass service remove one of the existing plate-glass windows so they could substitute it with a Lexan (a bulletproof

ABOVE: Working inside the Cobb Energy Performing Arts Centre proved challenging, as the production team could make very few changes to the existing structure for filming.

OPPOSITE: Special Effects Coordinator Darrell Pritchett, on ending the season with a bang: "I think we were able to come up with something that looked pretty darn good."

polycarbonate plastic) window the actors could pound on with axes and throw chairs at without causing damage.

"We couldn't do anything at that building, really, other than remove a window," explains Special Effects Coordinator Darrell Pritchett. "That was pretty much it. It's a very beautiful,

expensive complex there. Obviously, they did not want anything at all—they just weren't going to permit it. We were lucky to have the location, so most everything that you are seeing there are [visual effects] elements."

The grenade explosion was minor compared to the much bigger bang resulting from the self-destruct initiated by the CDC computer, which destroys the complex in a huge fireball. With all the sets and special effects in place, it was time for the visual effects team to come in and do their work. Of course, they'd already been dealing with that particular challenge for a few weeks.

"That was a huge undertaking, obviously," says Jason Sperling. "I think I'd first gotten wind that Frank was thinking of blowing up a CDC building midway through the first season—like episode 3—so we had about a couple of weeks [in] prepro to figure out how we were going to achieve this. Frank, to his credit, approved this amazing building that had just naturally a great look to it. For us, our challenge was trying to make that explosion convincing, beautiful, shocking, and devastating all in the same kind of sequence. We worked very closely with Darrell Pritchett to do the flame effects—the pyro effects—and all of the practical elements that we would need to enhance our digital 3-D building collapse."

"We did a day of elements shooting of different fire in different conditions and different setups," adds Pritchett. "Sam and Jason were involved in it. We went to one of their stages and did a bunch of fire stuff. Spent the entire day doing it different ways and they got some nice pieces that they were able to pop into the end and make it work."

Once they had a day's worth of recorded fire effects, they were only part of the way to the finished effect. As Sperling explains, "What you have there is a blending between the 3-D building which is being destroyed and the physics of it being simulated. Then you have the practical elements that we shot, basically just lining up our plates to the actual elements we would shoot pyro-wise. And then, seamlessly blending those together and trying to make that as devastating a scene as possible."

The visual effects team took extensive reference photos of the location so they had something to work with when rendering the building to which they would later add the pyro-effects. "The 3-D CGI guys—the modelers—model the building brick for brick," Sam Nicholson explains. "Then they do a collapse with all of the correct simulated dynamics of dust and bricks. So every single brick bounces and hits another brick—it's inverse kinematic–type math. On one hand, you have a completely virtual building collapsing. On the other hand, you have a real building that is doing absolutely nothing. The compositors put that together and you say, 'Okay, it either looks CG or we can see the blend.' Then everything in between the virtual space and the real space becomes element shooting."

To sell the shot, the team wanted fire to explode out of the windows and wrap around the tank and other vehicles in a realistic manner, which brought them back to their day of pyro-filming. "You have to believe the fire," Nicholson says. "If you don't believe the fire, then you're never going to believe the building. And so we shot the pyro with Darrell on a black stage where we had scale models of the building, the tanks, the vehicles, all these kinds of things, including the bodies on the ground—or rough approximations of them. Then you blow fire with propane mortars at high speed over those objects so that you really do get this gaseous explosive flame that comes out and wraps around the bodies. It's a physical thing. You're actually looking at fire doing what it's supposed to do—at a different scale and different speed—and then you shoot hundreds of those elements. You give those back to the compositors, [and] they blend them in."

But the work wasn't done there. The explosion doesn't just destroy the building and send flames and smoke out into the air. The environment around the building reacts as well. In the real world, a blast of that magnitude would affect the surrounding elements, blowing back the trees, for example. "So then we have to render a whole bunch of trees and use kinematics to blow the trees over and then go back and shoot fire that blows through the trees as another element."

A decade or so ago, this type of effect might have been done by blowing up a miniature scale model of the building. It would have been a more expensive process and one which would only happen once, since the model would be destroyed after the first take. The production would have to hope they had enough camera coverage to work with what they got. "Now, we have it happening in a three-dimensional environment," says Nicholson. "We can replay it, adjust it, pick our angles, and really perfect the shot. It's a combination of virtual reality and reality with a little bit of spice thrown in on the side."

Another one of the many elements added after principal photography is the musical score running beneath the scenes. Composer Bear McCreary was a perfect addition to *The Walking Dead* production team, not just because of his impressive résumé, but also for his familiarity with the source material. "I was a fan of the comic book before I began work on the series," McCreary proclaims. "At first that was very helpful, because I had a lot of enthusiasm and I knew a lot about the characters and I was very excited about it. But it also became detrimental because I was thinking ahead to problems that were not on my plate. I was thinking about character development that would not happen in that episode or wouldn't even happen this season, and for all we know, may not happen at all in the series."

McCreary soon discovered that in order to progress with his work on the episodes in front of him, he needed to tap into his enthusiasm for *The Walking Dead* comics, but set aside his knowledge of the existing story. "This is a separate interpretation," he explains. "This is a reinterpretation of these characters, and ultimately I am writing music for the show, not for the comic books. So, it was interesting. I didn't anticipate having that problem, but I found that to get started, I really did need to focus solely on the show, because I know the story so far down the line. I found it was not helping me to get ideas for the ninety-minute first episode and the six episodes that we've done."

Some television series rely heavily on music to interpret the action and characters with large orchestras or standout musical accompaniment which tells a story of its own in addition to the plot. *The Walking Dead* went in a different direction, taking a limited approach to the use of music, which was a strategy the composer and executive producers agreed on from the start. "I have a simple rule that if the scene does not need music, don't put music on it," says McCreary. "I approach everything that I score with this same mentality. If you go and look at certain episodes of *Battlestar Galactica* or *Terminator: The Sarah Connor Chronicles*, you will see a similar approach. With *The Walking Dead*, Frank Darabont and I were really on the same page from the beginning. This was always envisioned as a series that would use very little music."

The decision for a minimal score was for character-development reasons as well as narrative ones. Whenever possible, McCreary prefers to let the actors' performances tell their story. But from a narrative perspective, the score, or lack thereof, helps set the tone of the postapocalyptic world. "In setting a story like *The Walking Dead*, which focuses very much on the horror and the action and the suspense and the terror, people take for granted what a big component silence is in this equation," he says. "You've got a world where there are no more cell phones. There's no more radio. There's no more airplanes, buses, or trains. It's a very quiet world. And that's something we wanted to highlight in this series."

EPISODE 6: "TS-19"

Written by Adam Fierro and Frank Darabont
Directed by Guy Ferland

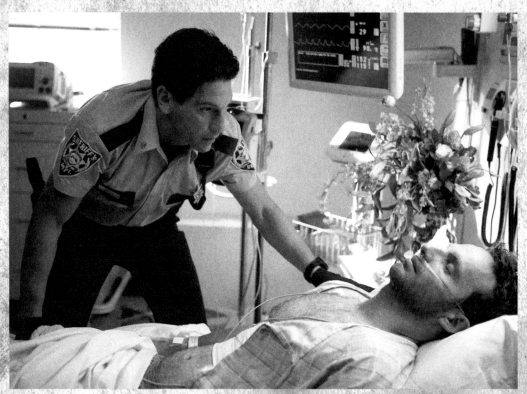

RICK: There's always hope. Maybe it won't be you, maybe not here, but
somebody, somewhere...

SYNOPSIS: A flashback reveals the fateful day when the Walkers overran the hospital where Rick lay in a coma and Shane was forced to make the difficult decision to leave him behind. But today, Rick leads the small group of survivors into the CDC where they meet the lone remaining scientist. Dr. Edwin Jenner insists the group submit to blood tests to make sure they are clear of infection before he agrees to allow them to stay.

The computer seals the facility and cuts the main power to the upper level as they head down to the underground bunker. Once all blood is cleared, they celebrate their survival with a hearty meal and copious amounts of wine. Shane brings the celebration to an abrupt end by demanding to know where all the other doctors went. This was the place that was supposed to be looking for a cure. It was their last salvation.

Jenner recounts the turmoil that occurred within the CDC after the outbreak. Some ran off. Others killed themselves. Only Jenner remained to keep working, hoping to do some good.

The doctor shows his guests to a section of the building that has not been powered down. As the group cleans up, Dale hears Andrea being sick in the bathroom. It's not the wine that's gotten to her. She's sickened by Jenner's revelation that all hope is gone.

In a private moment, Shane tries to convince Lori that he really believed Rick was dead when he convinced her to leave home. He pleads with her, wishing he could trade places with Rick both then and now, admitting that he loves Lori and trying to force her to do the same. His pleas grow aggressive, forcing Lori to slap him away, leaving scratch marks across his neck.

CONTINUED

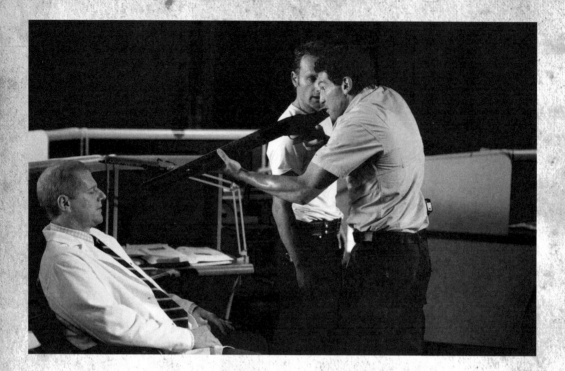

Everyone regrets the hard drinking the next morning, but no one more than Shane. Again, the lightheartedness is interrupted when Jenner is asked to explain what caused the outbreak. The doctor illustrates his story with an enhanced internal view of a body that had been infected: Test Subject 19. When the person was infected, the synapses in the brain shut down, causing death. Later, the synapses in the brain stem restarted, but the test subject was not alive.

The video plays out to the point when Jenner shot the patient in the head to end her reawakening. The CDC had no idea what caused this global epidemic, according to Jenner. There may be other facilities still working on the problem, but he doesn't know, since the infrastructure shut down a month earlier. But they have a more pressing issue to deal with. The computer is counting down until the facility runs out of power and

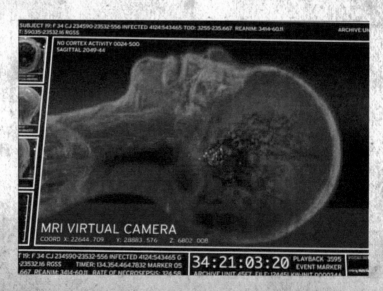

initiates a decontamination that will destroy the place and all the dangers it holds. The doors are sealed, as Jenner warned when they entered. In thirty minutes, everything will end.

Jenner is ready to die. Test Subject 19 was his wife, whom he promised he would keep searching for a cure as long as he could. Now that the end is near, he welcomes the explosion and can't understand why the rest of the group does not. Rick pleads with Jenner to let them out, and the man eventually relents, opening the lower doors for them..

Jacqui and Andrea don't want to leave, though. They prefer death to what waits outside. Dale stays behind with Andrea, trying to convince her that he needs her to live, as everyone else tries to get topside. As they leave, Jenner whispers something to Rick that hits him hard, but there is no time for a discussion.

Rick and the others try desperately to break out of the building, throwing everything they can at the bulletproof glass windows. Carol surprises everyone by pulling a grenade from her bag that she'd removed from Rick's clothes while doing his laundry. Rick had taken the weapon off the body of the dead soldier in the tank he found refuge in when he was attacked in downtown Atlanta. The grenade blast shatters the glass, allowing them to escape. Dale and Andrea flee the building behind them moments before it explodes. As the debris settles, the survivors ride off in search of a safe haven.

ABOVE: Existing offices in the convention center gave Jenner a space where he could isolate himself from the survivors.

In McCreary's earliest meetings with Hurd and Darabont, they spent a lot of time discussing the concept of soundlessness. "The idea is that the world they existed in is silent," he says. "So if you bring in a bunch of music and you play dramatic ambient music throughout the whole episode, you're damaging that. And you're taking away one of the things that make this world so creepy—which is its silence."

With the series conceived that way from the beginning, the composer knew exactly the moments where the music could come in and serve a very specific purpose. "It is the lack of music that ultimately becomes so effective and so terrifying," he continues. "It simultaneously scares us and informs us about the world that the characters inhabit. To me there was something very appealing about that."

McCreary also looked forward to playing up the horror element of the series. He knew that he needed to avoid a traditional approach to that type of score, because audiences have grown so familiar with the tricks of his trade. As McCreary explains, "Horror is a genre that has evolved a lot

musically in the past thirty years, and I've found that it's reached a point of audience saturation. What I mean by that is that audiences, no matter how hip they are to the horror genre, know what the musical tricks are. Horror has a long legacy of really powerful music."

He cites movies that have defined the genre like *Jaws*, *The Omen*, *The Shining*, and the scores of John Carpenter's films, which have set a tone that has been amplified over the years. "Throughout the '80s and the '90s, these same orchestral tricks started getting louder and louder and louder, and ultimately, I think audiences just got used to it," he says. "Horror today is a very difficult genre to write music in. What makes music scary? Unless you're four years old, you've probably heard all of the orchestral tricks that a composer has at his disposal."

Darabont and McCreary spent a lot of time figuring out ways to work around audience expectations. McCreary believes that all genres of music, but especially horror music, are relative to what the audience has been hearing up to that moment. If there is a subtle, ominous underscore playing during a scene, the traditional method to make the scene scarier is to simply make the music louder. "By having huge stretches of *The Walking Dead* be silent," he says, "we eliminate that problem. What happens is, there is no music. So if we want to create a scare, all we have to do is have music enter. It doesn't have to be loud, because there was no music. Any music is louder than no music."

This approach allows the composer to use very subtle gestures to achieve much bigger impact. "The score to *The Walking Dead* is actually quite small," he says. "It's performed by a very small orchestra—no more than ten players—and it's a very intimate sound. But on-screen it's very effective, because it comes after long stretches of silence. Rather than making this horror score louder and more aggressive and more dissonant than horror scores that you've heard in feature films in the past several decades, we went the other way, and made it smaller—which I think helps it stand out. It helps it feel a little different than the core music that an audience may be expecting."

Another important subject in McCreary's early meetings with the executive producers was the setting for the series. Having the show take place in the American South allowed the composer to set a specific tone and use nontraditional instruments. "I always like to use unusual instrumentation in my projects," he says. "I like to find a band of musicians to represent that project. For *The Walking Dead*, it was actually quite simple. The geographical location of the story has such a rich musical heritage to draw from. It would be foolish *not* to draw from it. But, it also was a challenge because the music that is coming from that area doesn't necessarily fit the tone of the series. We didn't want the score to sound like blues or bluegrass or zydeco, but elements from all of that music get pulled in. Then, what my job was to do was to distort, manipulate, and change these elements so that they are virtually unrecognizable to the casual listener."

ABOVE: The composer prefers to let the characters speak for themselves instead of relying on specific character themes to define them through music.

There's no better example of this than the inclusion of an electric banjo played by Steve Bartek, the lead guitarist of the cult rock band Oingo Boingo. McCreary works with Bartek on a lot of his projects, and the two spent some time talking about how to find this sound. They ran the music of the electric banjo through distortion pedals and effects processors to create a sound that didn't resemble the instrument at all. They now had a sound they could feature, although it wasn't quite a perfect fit yet.

"I really needed to get Steve, as a player, in the mood of the show," McCreary adds. "I would have him play banjo licks over some of these suspense scenes, and he just sounded too good because he's such a good guitarist. Finally, I told him to start imagining that he is actually a banjo player who was bitten by a zombie and has become a zombie. I told him to close his eyes and imagine that he wakes up and he's a member of the living undead, but he still has his banjo strapped to his body. His decaying hands reach up to the instrument and start plucking on the strings using nothing but muscle memory, because there's no mind there anymore. I asked him, 'What does that sound like?' And he thought about it and he started playing his banjo, and it was perfect. That is the sound that you hear throughout the whole score."

Beyond the electric banjo, McCreary stocks his score with a lot of Autoharp and Appalachian dulcimer, two instruments often associated with folk music. "They have a timbre that I liked, but the chord wasn't too pleasing," he says. "There's no way to create really dissonant, angular music on them without detuning them

ABOVE: The Southern setting of the comic book and TV series inspires many of the music choices for the episodes.

OPPOSITE: The dramatic elements of the series did not match the more upbeat rhythms of Southern music, but McCreary was able to take those sounds and filter them for the serious tone of the scenes.

substantially. So one of the things that I did was we found some old Autoharps that were beyond repair, and we detuned them even further and created these sounds that were like these horrible, scraping noises with just the slightest little taste of pitch. There's almost no pitch at all—it's almost a percussion instrument. . . . It creates a terrifying sound that is somehow evocative of folk music. It literally sounds like the music itself is undead. It sounds like bluegrass, folk, country-western, zydeco music has risen from the dead, and this is what it sounds like. Which was really fun for me on an intellectual and conceptual level—to be able to think about music in this way. There are very few projects that would ever give me the leeway to do that."

EIGHT

BRING OUT YOUR DEAD:

MARKETING THE SERIES

The ninety-minute pilot was set to premiere in the United States on October 31, 2010, as part of the Fearfest block of AMC's Halloween programming. Anticipation had already been building among the comic readership from the moment the series was announced, but the network needed to capitalize on that buzz and promote the show to potential viewers unfamiliar with the comic. While episodes of *The Walking Dead* were still being filmed, AMC began the marketing push.

The main marketing campaign image of Rick on horseback riding into Atlanta grew out of a brief scene from the pilot episode that perfectly encapsulated the theme of the series for both established fans as well as the uninitiated. "I have to say, that was brilliant on AMC's part," notes Robert Kirkman. "I was very concerned, when they were putting the show together, that they would use the zombies in marketing. I think that the charm of the show is that it is about the characters, and it would be unfortunate if the marketing was all, 'Here's a zombie trying to eat you!' The fact that they picked a guy on a horse riding into Atlanta—and you couldn't really see any zombies, which made it about a person dealing with the end of the world—I think that was really smart on AMC's part. I think that got a lot of people interested in the show."

Gale Anne Hurd agrees that it was the right image both for the episode and the marketing. "The pilot is very much one man's journey," she says. "There is almost a western sensibility to it; that lone sheriff riding into town, riding into hostile territory. And yet this is as contemporary a tale as you could possibly tell. That one image is so iconic. You really get that there's this incredible devastation. You've got lines of cars and buses burned out, stopped, destroyed. You can see buildings that are destroyed. What do you do in a world like that? Well, in this case, with gas in such short supply, you revert [and the world shifts] to a post-digital world; post-everything that we take for granted in this world: post-Internet, post-vehicle, post–any kind of transportation. That one image sold it completely. We've got the sheriff and he's riding into town and he's all alone. You didn't need zombies."

The journey to adapt the artwork of Rick riding into Atlanta from page to screen that

ABOVE: The lone lawman rides into Atlanta on horseback in issue no. 2, page 9, panel 1.

ABOVE: The visual effects team combined numerous separate images into one final composite of Rick riding into Atlanta.

PREVIOUS SPREAD: The AMC marketing team adapted what appeared onscreen, enhancing the artwork to emphasize the desolation of the series.

would later inspire the marketing campaign required a substantial amount of visual effects work. Although it only appeared for a few seconds in the pilot episode, the moment was important enough for the series overall to easily justify the amount of time and effort the visual effects team put into creating the scene.

Jason Sperling, who was a huge fan of the comic long before he started working on the series, understood the importance of capturing that image properly. It was an interesting challenge for the visual effects team, as it was composed entirely of disparate elements. "We worked very closely with our matte painters to start with the comic book panel as the inspiration, but then take it to the next degree," Sperling explains. "All the little touches that we put in there to try to make that scene feel more realistic and [for] the weight of that scene to really hit you—storm clouds, birds on the horizon circling what you would think would be their dinner, and the isolation of Rick himself as he walks in against this looming skyline—I think they really [catch] what the course of *The Walking Dead* series will be, which is about human isolation in this new world."

Sam Nicholson describes the images as a massive photo collage blended with matte painting. He breaks down some of the various elements: "Rick's shot in a parking lot because we could get the correct angle on him, but he's just against cement. So, he's one element. Then we went out and shot the freeway—obviously with a lot of cars on it—with still cameras and motion picture cameras and all that kind of stuff. And that's another element. Then we shot the buildings, which is another element. And then we shot the skies, another element. And the birds, another element."

Both Nicholson and Sperling credit Frank Darabont's artistic vision as uniting the entire scene for them, with minimal complications. "He's very articulate and very precise in his comments," says Nicholson. "He has a very clear-cut idea off the top. It allows us as visual effects artists to really finely hone in on the focus of a final shot, and not swerve this direction and that direction, back and forth—because you wind up with seventy revisions to a shot. I think we revised that one maybe forty or fifty times to get it right. But in each of those sessions you're saying, 'Well, the birds are too distracting, let's back them off,' or, 'The birds come forward too much, put them in depth more.' Some of it is just artistic perspective, and some of it is 'Where does your eye go in the frame?' Anything that is distracting to him—even every single piece of trash that blows across the road—is shot separately against green screen and calculated and put in. When you look at the shot you say, 'Do we have too much trash? Does it distract from Rick? Where does your eye go?' It's kind of like a visual exercise."

Nicholson believes that they viewed that shot about five hundred times with something like fifty people involved each time. "So you've got thousands of eyeballs looking at this thing again, again, and again to say, 'Where does your eye go? What is the purpose of the shot? Does it tell a story? Does the shot itself have a beginning, middle, and end?' Like a good script, good shot design needs to have a beginning, middle, and end, and has to tell the story. It has to enhance the story. If you get it just right after all that, it becomes an iconic image, and suddenly it represents the entire show. That is what we would consider a very successful shot. So, we're very happy about it."

AMC was happy about it, too, and took the image even further to create the final key art.

Linda Schupack, senior vice president of marketing for AMC, explains: "For our key art, we look to showcase an iconic image that speaks to the themes and story of the series. In this case, Rick on horseback, riding into Atlanta down an empty highway with abandoned cars strewn in the opposite lane, set up the story of survival and the central question of how you hold on to your humanity amidst a zombie apocalypse. The color palette also established an uneasy moodiness."

The overriding marketing image might not have had a single zombie in it, but that was not the entire campaign. AMC knew that revealing the zombies of *The Walking Dead* was an important element to bring fans of the genre on board, but they also needed to be practical in their approach. Conveniently, there was the powerful pilot teaser image of the hospital doors padlocked shut and painted with a warning of the dead inside. Again, this image expanded on the comic book artwork. In the commercials those doors breathed open as the zombie threat pressed against them. The creatures themselves were not kept hidden until the series revealed them, but they were used minimally in the advertising to hold to the human focus of the show.

"Our marketing and on-air teams planned and executed a really thoughtful strategy, targeting genre fans, as well as the broader, core drama audience," explains Charlie Collier, president of AMC. "There was never any doubt that the 'zombie fan' would have plenty to sink his

OPPOSITE: Additional key art advertising the series used zombie imagery, though these ads were not as prevalent as the main promotional image of Rick riding into Atlanta.

THE WALKING DEAD

A NEW ORIGINAL SERIES COMING THIS OCTOBER

aMC®

amcthewalkingdead.com

teeth into (sorry) here, but the marketing brilliance came in making sure many non-zombie viewers who loved drama and engaging stories of survival would be captivated by this unique storytelling as well. From the hard-core fan at Comic-Con to a more casual on-air drama event viewer, leading up to the premiere, we used every resource we could muster to let people know a special television event was coming to AMC on Halloween night."

Those hardcore fans of Comic-Con were certainly not forgotten. The annual convention in San Diego attracts approximately 125,000 fans a day and it has become a prime destination for comic book publishers as well as movie studios and TV networks wanting to roll out their product to a targeted demographic. As a television show built off a popular comic book, it was imperative that *The Walking Dead* make a splash at the 2010 Comic-Con, and it did not fail to impress. Schupack believes that a presence at the annual convention was key to marketing the series. "We wanted to ignite this super passionate fan base first, get them excited by what they were seeing and then gradually broaden our marketing efforts."

"I thought the Comic-Con push was great," says Executive Producer David Alpert. "It's the army of the faithful. It's the legions of fanboys and the passionate people. Honestly, it's where Robert and I come from. It's sort of our passion and our background—for Robert obviously more than me—but there's something really pure. There's no love like geek love. . . . To see the reactions those people had. They were there because they had read the book and loved the

book. And they were there because . . . this was something by one of their own, for them."

Over the four-day weekend, Kirkman appeared on three panels devoted to *The Walking Dead* and his other comic book work. Of the three, the panel specifically focused on the new television series (during which he shared the dais with the show's cast and other producers) was one of the most popular events of the weekend. The fan reaction was a particular highlight for Alpert to witness, having worked with Kirkman on the business side of the comic book series for years.

"There are plenty of shows and movies out there now that feel intentionally marketed or manipulated to appeal to audiences," Alpert notes. "Whereas this one they knew—because of the people involved, because of all of the big names involved, but also because of the book—they knew that it was going to be something special. To see that reaction when there had been no footage released up until that point—we filled that hall in two seconds with people just off of the fact that this was being made. And that's amazing."

AMC's presence at the convention was not limited to that one panel. The booth they set up on the main floor was one of the most talked-about sights of the convention. The network pulled out all the stops with their presentation, going so far as to bring to life the farmhouse set where Rick sees the remains of a family that took their lives rather than suffering through the zombie apocalypse.

"The farmhouse set was the first thing we shot," says Production Designer Greg Melton.

ABOVE and FOLLOWING SPREAD: The interior of the farmhouse from issue no. 2 was re-created for the series, then parts of the set were shipped to San Diego Comic-Con for display.

"We used an existing farm out near Mansfield, Georgia. It laid out nicely for Rick to pass by windows and come upon this grisly scene. We redressed the living room and added the blood-stained wall. We were still shooting when I was contacted about helping re-create it for Comic-Con. All the set dressing was shipped to San Diego, along with paint samples."

"We wanted to allow people to 'enter' the world of *The Walking Dead*," Schupack explains. "We created a tableau where, at first glance, it looks like home—and then you realize the world has been totally upended. We worked with the crew of *The Walking Dead* to replicate the scene and Greg Nicotero provided the 'dead farmer' and his wife from the pilot. The response we received—from our panel featuring the cast, Frank, Gale and Robert, and our on-site zombie activations and the booth—was

so overwhelmingly positive that we knew from that point on that we were in for a truly wild ride."

Luckily, San Diego isn't the only city to host a comic book convention, and the cast and crew have made appearances at various venues throughout the year. It is an experience that Chandler Riggs has enjoyed immensely. "We have seen great costumes at cons and been interviewed a lot," he says. "Everyone is really nice, and some artists have even given me drawings they did of me. Signing autographs, hearing other people's opinions about the show, and just looking at the other things at the conventions is so much fun!"

Another cast member enjoying the convention circuit is Steven Yeun. The actor laments the fact that he never made it to San Diego Comic-Con before the series launched, but he

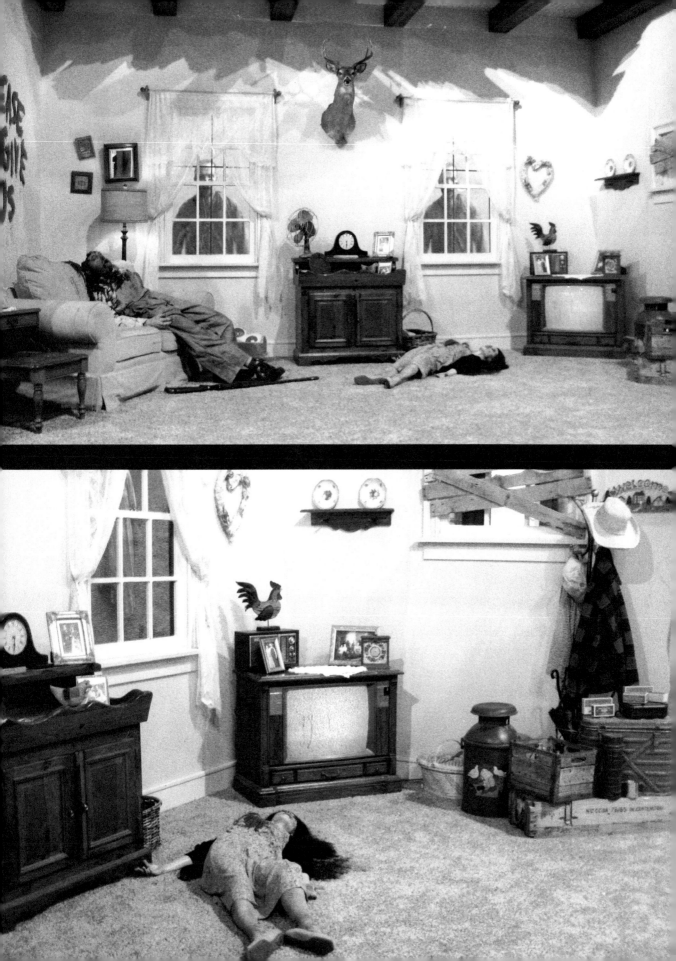

wasn't planning to miss the opportunity again. "The fans are great," he says. "They are all so excited about the show. It's good to see and hear. The conventions are great as well. You get to see the people firsthand who are keeping you on the air."

As the premiere date approached, one last piece of viral marketing would come, in the form of a World Zombie Invasion.

To celebrate the upcoming series premiere in the U.S. and abroad, AMC worked in conjunction with FOX International to stage a zombie invasion "flash mob" in twenty-six major cities around the world. According to the network, it was the first time anyone had tried to pull off a global activation of that magnitude. Zombies were set up with a team of photographers and videographers in dozens of cities around the world. Their activities were carefully choreographed and times so that digital uploads of the imagery of the event could be posted as the invasion made its way around the world. It started at dawn in cities to signify the dawning of the zombie apocalypse and take advantage of weekend morning commuters. Through the online posts about the event people could witness it as it moved through the various time zones.

"We loved the global zombie 'commute,'" says Schupack: "We worked very closely with our foreign distributor, Fox International, and started the 'infestation' at dawn in Taipei and Hong Kong and ended in Los Angeles at the AMC premiere. In each market we had photographers and video crews quickly uploading the images that best represented the invasion in their city whether it be London, Istanbul, Madrid, Rome, Athens, Belgrade, Johannesburg or Buenos Aires. The promotion laid the foundation establishing *The Walking Dead* as a global phenomenon."

The American premiere of the series was scheduled to cap off the network's signature Halloween-time programming. Collier explains, "One of AMC's highest-rated movie events every year, for each of the last fourteen years, is our two-week commitment to the best films in the horror world. Each Halloween season, AMC creates a virtual film festival on-air and online in an event we call Fearfest. On Sunday, October 31, 2010, that film event— and, obviously, the pop-culture event that is Halloween—served to support the premiere of the AMC original series *The Walking Dead*.

The Walking Dead premiere episode was the highest rated debut ever on AMC, drawing 5.3 million total viewers and the series went on to become the most-watched basic cable television series of 2010 among adults in the 18-49 demographic. The show was a critical success as well, receiving multiple award nominations and being named as one of the top ten television programs of 2010 by the American Film Institute. AMC's senior vice-president of original programming, production, and digital content Joel Stillerman is proud of the show's success that transcend merely demographic numbers. "It became something that felt like an event that you really had to watch," he notes. "*The Walking Dead* touched a nerve culturally, and that is just as important to us as ratings."

TO BE CONTINUED . . .

ABOVE: As with the second arc of the comic book series, the second season of *The Walking Dead* will find the survivors riding off into the future in search of a safe haven.

As flames and smoke rise from the remains of the CDC building at the end of season 1, Rick, Lori, and the rest of the survivors take off in their caravan for destinations unknown. While, certainly, these characters do not know what lies ahead of them, the audience already has some clues, depending on how closely the series will follow the source material in the second season and beyond. As Frank Darabont has said, the writers will follow Robert Kirkman's path, but diverge every now and again to explore new plotlines and meet new characters. As for any specifics about the second season, the production team is unsurprisingly tight-lipped, but they do have some hints . . .

FRANK DARABONT: The zombie set pieces will happen. The zombies will break through the door. There will be those great scenes and the exploding heads, but that's not what I'm thinking about for a second season. I'm thinking about those characters. I'm thinking about those people. What do they go through? Andrea's lost somebody very dear to her, and what does that mean to her? What about the relationship with this man who's this sort of father figure to her?

GALE ANNE HURD: Rick—as we have seen in the first season, and we'll see even more so in the second season—has to make very, very difficult decisions. He has to do what he thinks is right. Many times in the first season, we've seen that those decisions may not have been the right ones, but he certainly made those choices for all the right reasons.

ROBERT KIRKMAN: I think that when people see season 2, they'll see that keeping Shane alive was the best decision. It's going to lead to some really rich, interesting stories. That's the stuff that really makes me excited about the TV show. Seeing a character like Shane interact with Hershel when we get to Hershel's farm is going to be so much fun, because those two never met or interacted in the comic book. So, while we're going to be doing stories from the comic book, exactly as they happen in the comic book to a certain extent, there's that x-factor. There's that extra character who wasn't there before, and it changes things in ways that are really unexpected. I think that that's going to make season 2, in particular, really exciting for all the comic book fans, because they're going to get the stuff that they want to see, but they're going to see it in such a different way. I think it will surprise some people.

FRANK DARABONT: I can't wait to meet The Governor. I can't wait to get into that whole story line. I can't wait to bring Michonne into it and Tyreese and these characters, because they're so indelible. They made such a huge impact on us, on the readership of the comic book. These are the characters we dug the most. Of course, I can't wait to get to those characters and those story lines, because they're going to be tremendously fun to explore on-screen and through the process of developing the teleplays.

CHARLIE ADLARD: I am looking forward to Michonne being introduced. . . . It will be fantastic to see what they do with my stuff, bringing in the characters that I created.

STEVEN YEUN: I think what's going to be great, with the addition of Maggie, is she is going to be a huge catalyst for Glenn's growth and transformation. Before Maggie, he kind of saw himself as expendable, as someone who can put his neck out on the line, because then he can go out in a blaze of glory while clearing his conscience about not doing anything during the "normal" world. But I think with Maggie, he sees her as a sole reason to live. That is huge.

CHANDLER RIGGS: Two things I am looking forward to are getting the hat and getting shot. I would like to shoot some zombies soon. Of course I have no idea what they will really do.

Although the final plots won't be revealed until the second season airs, there are definite clues from the comic book about the many different twists and turns the television series could take. . . .

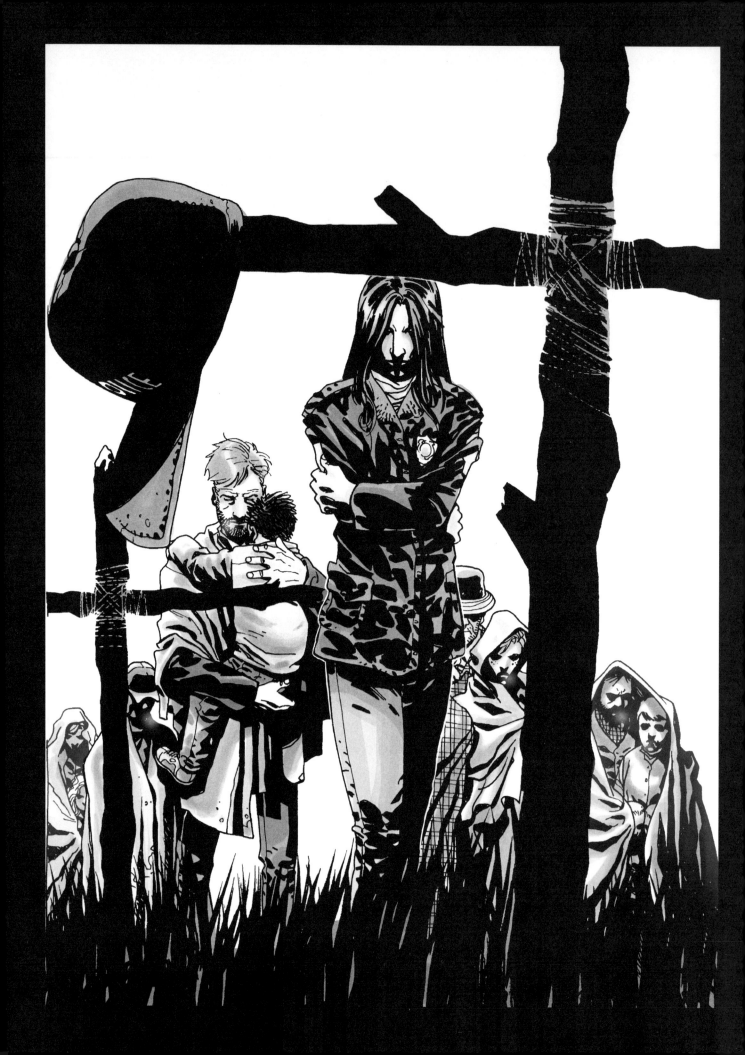

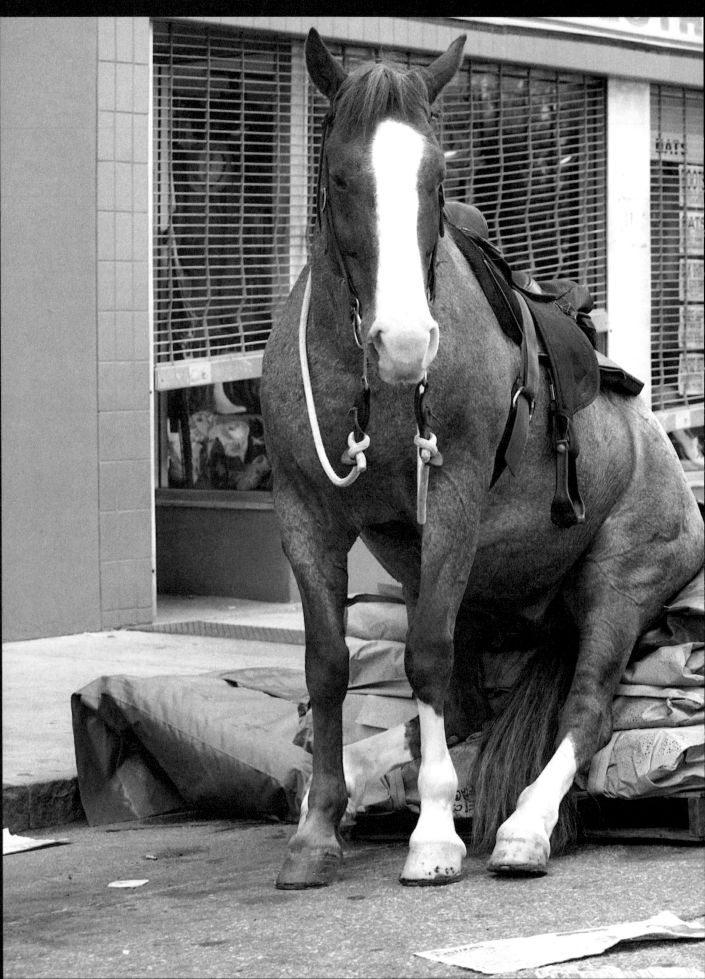

Editor: Eric Klopfer
Designers: Kris Tobiassen and Danielle Young
Production Manager: Anet Sirna-Bruder

Library of Congress Cataloging-in-Publication Data

Ruditis, Paul.
  The walking dead chronicles : the official companion
book / by Paul
Ruditis ; introduction by Robert Kirkman.
     p. cm.
  ISBN 978-1-4197-0119-1
  1. Walking dead (Television program) I. Title.
  PN1992.77.W25R74 2011
  791.45'72—dc23
                              2011027071

Abrams books are available at special discounts when
purchased in quantity for premiums and promotions as
well as fundraising or educational use. Special editions
can also be created to specification. For details, contact
specialsales@abramsbooks.com or the address below.

ABRAMS
THE ART OF BOOKS SINCE 1949

115 West 18th Street
New York, NY 10011
www.abramsbooks.com

Frank Darabont interview material provided by
Constantine Nasr

All live-action images and materials related to AMC's
The Walking Dead copyright © 2010 AMC Film
Holdings LLC. All rights reserved.
All comic book images and materials related to AMC's
The Walking Dead copyright © 2010 Robert Kirkman.
Photography by Scott Garfield/AMC and Matthew
Welch/AMC.

All images courtesy of AMC and Robert Kirkman, with
the exception of the following:
Pages 46, 59 (bottom), 61 (top left and bottom right),
62 (all), 63, 70, 72, 73 (all), 78, 79 (bottom), 80 (both), 86,
138, and 157 (all): Courtesy of KNB EFX Group, Inc.

Pages 64 (all), 82, 122 (all), 132 (bottom left and bottom
right), 135 (all), 154 (all), 155 (all), 176 (all), and 191 (all):
Courtesy of Stargate Studios

ACKNOWLEDGMENTS

My heartfelt gratitude and appreciation go out to everyone
that contributed to this book:

   To Frank Darabont, Gale Anne Hurd, Robert
Kirkman, David Alpert, Charlie Adlard, Eric Stephenson,
Sina Grace, Greg Nicotero, and the entire cast and crew
of *The Walking Dead*, especially Jeffrey DeMunn, Steven
Yeun, Chandler Riggs and the Riggs family, Sharon Bialy,
David Boyd, Jess Clark, Alex Hajdu, Phillip Kobylanski,
Greg Melton, Bear McCreary, Sam Nicholson, Darrell
Pritchett, Jason Sperling, David Tattersall, and Sherry
Thomas.

   To everyone associated with AMC, especially Charlie
Collier, Joel Stillerman, Linda Schupack, and Theresa
Beyer, and to Striker Entertainment's Cambria Beauvais.

   To the editor that guided me through the land of
the dead, Eric Klopfer, along with everyone at Abrams,
including Lindley Boegehold, Michelle Ishay, Michael
Jacobs, Ivy McFadden, Anet Sirna-Bruder, Steve Tager,
and designers Kris Tobiassen and Danielle Young.

   To Tim Gaskill and Phyllis Ungerleider for their
timely assistance on the project and, especially, to Paula
Block and Terry Erdmann for always keeping me in mind.
   I thank you.

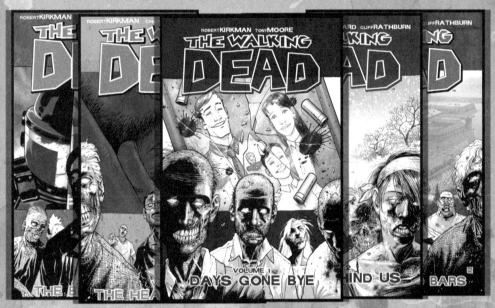

THE
WALKING DEAD

"...surprisingly scary and remarkably good..."
-The New York Times

NEW SEASON
PREMIERES OCT 16
aMC
SUNDAYS 9/8c